vehicle maintenance for women

First published in 2004 by Cassell Illustrated
A Member of Octopus Publishing Group Ltd.
2-4 Heron Quays
London
E14 4JP

ISBN 1-84403-258-2

Conceived, designed and produced by
Quid Publishing
Fourth Floor
Sheridan House
112-116 Western Road
Hove BN3 1DD
England
www.quidpublishing.com

Author: Charlotte Williamson
Publisher: Nigel Browning
Publishing Manager: Sophie Martin
Design and Project Management: Essential Works
Illustrations: Matt Pagett

Printed and bound in China by Regent Publishing Services

NOTE
Every effort has been taken to ensure that all information in this book is correct and compatible with national standards at the time of publication. This book is not intended to replace manufacturers' instructions in the use of their tools or products - always follow their safety guidelines.
The author, publisher and copyright holder assume no responsibility for any injury, loss or damage caused or sustained as a consequence of the use and application of the contents of this book.

vehicle
maintenance
for women

CONTENTS

4 Wheels

2 Wheels

Pedal Power

The Art and Science of Vehicle Maintenance

First, let's dispel those myths. Women are bad drivers. Wrong: women are not as reckless as men, are less likely to be involved in a head-on collision, and account for a mere two per cent of convictions for dangerous driving.

Women don't have mechanical brains. Wrong: more women are training to be mechanics than ever before – in fact, the number of women on some courses has more than tripled in the past few years.

Women are afraid to peek under the bonnet when something goes awry. Wrong: women today are much more comfortable with cars, and the same goes for motorcycles and bicycles. This is partly because (and we're excluding cycles here) the electronic age has overtaken the mechanical, so most repairs no longer require the arduous task – that only a man could enjoy – of stripping an engine and gearbox. And anyway, like most male-dominated areas of 'expertise' (DIY is another classic case), vehicle maintenance is very methodical. And not very hard.

But where to start? This is where **Vehicle Maintenance for Women** comes in. Split into cars, motorcycles and bikes, this book will guide you through basic maintenance and basic repairs, such as when to attempt a job yourself, what tools to use and when to contact a professional mechanic. We will also explain what all the different components are called and how they work, so if you do visit a garage (often a testosterone-fuelled environment, think Danny and the T-Birds in *Grease*), you won't be dismissed as a fluffy airhead – and hopefully won't get conned.

We will also offer crucial advice on essential checks before setting off, how to drive in difficult weather conditions, how to handle an accident or a breakdown and what to do when travelling abroad. We'll help you with just about everything, in fact, bar how to actually drive – but since you're a woman, you'll be good at that already.

This book is aimed at women drivers and riders of all ages and abilities. One motoring organisation reckons that a lack of basic vehicle maintenance is behind at least half of all breakdowns it is called to. If repairs seem too daunting, though, just knowing how to check your basics – oil, water, tyres, whatever – will put you in good stead.

So keep this guide handy, in your glove box or your pannier, and if something goes wrong, reach for **Vehicle Maintenance for Women** instead of your boyfriend's phone number. After all, if it's not too difficult for men . . .

GREASY GLORIA

Meet Greasy Gloria. She's been there, done that, and knows her seat belt from her fan belt better than any man. Gloria's tips will keep you on the road – and on your toes.

Do you know it all already?

Probably not, since you bought this book, but have a go at this quick questionnaire anyway to see how much of a clever-clogs you really are. Answers are at the back (page 144). Don't cheat, now.

WHAT IS A SALOON?

A) A TYPE OF CAR DISTINGUISHED BY ITS SEPARATE BOOT
B) A TYPE OF CAR DISTINGUISHED BY ITS COMBINED REAR SEATS AND BOOT
C) A TYPE OF CAR WITH ONLY THREE DOORS (INCLUDING BOOT)
D) A TYPE OF CAR WITH ONLY TWO SEATS
E) THE BEST PLACE TO GET A HAIRCUT

FROM WHAT IS COOLANT COMPOSED?

A) ONE-THIRD WATER AND TWO-THIRDS ANTI-FREEZE
B) HALF WATER, HALF ANTI-FREEZE
C) ONE-THIRD ANTI-FREEZE AND TWO-THIRDS WATER
D) ANTI-FREEZE, NO WATER
E) VODKA AND CRANBERRY JUICE

HOW OFTEN SHOULD YOU CLEAN YOUR MOTORCYCLE?

A) DAILY
B) WEEKLY
C) FORTNIGHTLY
D) MONTHLY
E) ONLY WHEN IT'S REALLY MUDDY

WHAT DOES AN ODOMETER MEASURE?

A) SPEED
B) THE NUMBER OF KILOMETRES/MILES A CAR HAS DRIVEN
C) FUEL CONSUMPTION
D) TEMPERATURE
E) WHEN TO CHANGE THE AIR CONDITIONER

WHAT'S THE BEST BRUSH FOR CLEANING A BICYCLE?

A) A PAINTBRUSH
B) A CARPET BRUSH
C) A HAIRBRUSH
D) A TOOTHBRUSH
E) ALL OF THE ABOVE

WHAT IS A TORQUE WRENCH?

A) A TOOL THAT MAKES A LOUD CLICK WHEN THE CORRECT AMOUNT OF PRESSURE IS APPLIED TO A NUT AND BOLT
B) A TOOL THAT MAKES NO SOUND WHEN THE CORRECT AMOUNT OF PRESSURE IS APPLIED TO A NUT AND BOLT
C) A DEVICE FOR DRIVING-IN SCREWS
D) A TYPE OF HAMMER
E) NONE OF THE ABOVE

WHAT ARE THE BEST SHOES FOR CYCLING?

A) PUMPS
B) BROGUES
C) TRAINERS
D) PLATFORMS
E) STILETTOS

WHEN CARRYING A PASSENGER ON A MOTORCYCLE, WHAT'S THE MOST IMPORTANT PIECE OF INFORMATION TO TELL THEM ABOUT BEFORE SETTING OFF?

A) LEAN INTO BENDS
B) WATCH OUT FOR THE FLIES
C) WAVE AT OTHER RIDERS
D) HOLD ON ONLY IF YOU FEEL LIKE IT
E) DON'T ENVY OTHER PASSENGERS IN SIDECARS

What To Do When

Good maintenance is all about being super-organised. If the thought of checking your vehicle's road-worthiness thoroughly overwhelms you, dole out your TLC in stages to halt any 'Crumbs! I haven't cleaned my car for two years!' panic attacks.

That means keeping a schedule. Don't wait until a situation is out of control – the tyre treads are worn down to the ground, for instance. Leaving problem areas lingering will increase the depreciation on your vehicle and is also how accidents happen. For pointers, consult the charts for what to do when.

Vehicles need different degrees of maintenance according to the season. Rain can leave you with a muddy bike, for instance, and one that will need attending to immediately after a journey unless you want to start riding a rust bucket. Likewise, ensure that your car contains windscreen washer fluid appropriate for the correct season.

Before you start

Invest in a good-quality tool kit. Each vehicle section of this book contains a list of what you'll need for basic home maintenance, but in general you should include the following: screwdrivers (both flat-blade and Phillips), pliers, and spanners in differing sizes. You will also need a handful of clean rags, a set of overalls/clothes you don't mind ruining, and a variety of cleansers and waxes.

And don't forget the paperwork

Yes, admin is a bore, but always remember to update your insurance and any vehicle or road tax renewals. And take any motor vehicles to a garage for an annual service. Your vehicle maintenance mantra should be thus: don't think of a routine as something you're a slave to. Instead consider it something you have control over, thereby empowering both you and your vehicle. Very self-helpy, but it works!

Cars Chore Chart

DAILY:

- INSPECT FOR FLAT TYRES
- WALK AROUND THE CAR AND ENSURE NOTHING IS DAMAGED, PAYING SPECIAL ATTENTION TO BOTH FRONT AND REAR LIGHTS
- CHECK THE LIGHTS AND INDICATORS ARE WORKING CORRECTLY
- MAKE SURE WINDSCREENS AND WINDOWS ARE CLEAN
- TEST THE BRAKES WORK BY SQUEEZING THE PEDAL SHORTLY AFTER DRIVING OFF

WEEKLY:

- CHECK THE FUEL LEVEL – THIS SHOULD ALWAYS BE ABOVE THE HALFWAY MARK – AND LOOK FOR ANY LEAKS
- INSPECT THE OIL; AGAIN, THIS SHOULD BE ABOVE THE HALFWAY MARK ON THE DIPSTICK. ALSO LOOK FOR LEAKS
- CHECK THE BRAKE AND CLUTCH FLUID AND LOOK FOR LEAKS
- EXAMINE THE COOLANT LEVEL – THIS SHOULD BE DONE WHEN THE ENGINE IS COLD. AND AGAIN, LOOK FOR LEAKS
- MAKE SURE THERE'S SUFFICIENT FLUID IN THE WINDSCREEN WASHER RESERVOIR
- ASK SOMEONE TO HELP YOU CHECK THE BRAKE LIGHTS
- CHECK THE BATTERY CONNECTIONS ARE TIGHT AND CLEAN AND TOP UP WITH DISTILLED WATER – NEVER TAP – IF NECESSARY (YOU WON'T HAVE TO DO THIS IF THE BATTERY IS SEALED)

MONTHLY:

- TEST YOUR TYRES' PRESSURE WHEN THEY ARE COLD – AND DON'T FORGET THE SPARE. ALSO CHECK THE TYRE TREAD
- MAKE SURE THE FAN BELT IS SUFFICIENTLY TIGHT AND IS NOT WORN
- CHECK THE WIPER BLADES; REPLACE IF WORN
- GIVE THE CAR A GOOD CLEAN AND POLISH
- IF YOU NORMALLY ONLY USE THE CAR FOR SHORT TRIPS, TAKE IT OUT ON A LONGER RUN. THIS IS GOOD FOR THE ENGINE AND RECHARGES THE BATTERY

AND EVERY SIX MONTHS OR SO:

- CHECK COMPONENTS – AIR FILTER, FUEL FILTER AND SPARK PLUGS SHOULD BE CHANGED AT THE SERVICE INTERVALS RECOMMENDED IN YOUR HANDBOOK. THIS SHOULD BE CARRIED OUT WHEN YOU TAKE YOUR CAR IN FOR ITS SERVICE

Motorcycles Chore Chart

DAILY:
- TEST ALL THE LIGHTS: FRONT, REAR, SIDE, BOTH INDICATORS AND BRAKE
- CHECK THE CHAIN IS SECURE
- MAKE SURE THE TYRES CONTAIN NO STRAY DEBRIS LIKE NAILS OR STONES
- TEST THAT THE BRAKES WORK BY SQUEEZING THE FRONT BRAKE LEVER
- CHECK THE FUEL AND OIL

WEEKLY:
- EXAMINE THE DRIVE CHAIN: IT SHOULD BE NEITHER TOO SLACK NOR TOO TIGHT
- CHECK THE STEERING HEAD BEARINGS FOR SMOOTH STEERING MOVEMENT. IF THE ADJUSTMENT IS WONKY, YOUR BIKE WILL BE DIFFICULT TO CONTROL
- TEST YOUR TYRES' PRESSURE AND TREAD
- CHECK YOUR HORN'S HOOTING, ALTHOUGH NOT AT 2AM IN A RESIDENTIAL AREA
- MAKE SURE EVERY VISIBLE NUT AND BOLT IS TIGHT

FORTNIGHTLY:
- TEST THE SUSPENSION BY SITTING ON THE BIKE AND BOUNCING UP AND DOWN
- GIVE THE BATTERY A ONCE-OVER
- CHECK FOR ANY OIL LEAKING FROM THE SHOCK ABSORBERS AND FRONT FORKS
- INSPECT THE THROTTLE – THAT IT CLOSES PROPERLY WHEN RELEASED AND THAT THE CABLES AREN'T FRAYED
- IF THE CLUTCH IS HYDRAULICALLY OPERATED, CHECK THE FLUID LEVEL AND LOOK FOR ANY LEAKS
- CHECK BRAKE FLUID LEVEL AND PADS
- FOR LIQUID-COOLED ENGINES, CHECK THE COOLANT LEVEL IS BETWEEN MIN/MAX
- IF YOUR BIKE HAS A STAND, CHECK THE WHEELS ARE RUNNING CORRECTLY BY SPINNING EACH ONE ROUND
- CHECK THE AIR FILTER – REPLACE IT AT THE RECOMMENDED INTERVALS
- CLEAN YOUR BIKE

Bicycles Chore Chart

WEEKLY:
- CHECK THE BRAKES. RIDE A FEW METRES THEN GIVE THEM A GOOD SQUEEZE – YOU SHOULD ONLY HAVE TO PULL HALFWAY DOWN FOR THEM TO PROPERLY WORK. IF THEY'RE NOT WORKING, DON'T USE THE BIKE
- CHECK THE TYRES' PRESSURE AND GIVE THEM THE ONCE-OVER FOR STRAY DEBRIS SUCH AS NAILS
- MAKE SURE THE SPOKES AREN'T DAMAGED AND THAT THE WHEELS ARE 'TRUE' AND CORRECTLY ALIGNED
- TEST THE LIGHTS
- CHECK THE BELL
- CHECK THE SADDLE IS TIGHT – THERE SHOULD BE NO MOVEMENT
- GIVE THE BIKE A QUICK ALL-OVER WIPE WITH A CLOTH

FORTNIGHTLY:
- MAKE SURE THE CHAIN IS OILED AND PROPERLY ADJUSTED
- LOOK AT THE BRAKE PADS (THE PART OF BRAKE THAT TOUCHES THE WHEEL RIM WHEN THE BRAKE LEVER IS APPLIED). THERE SHOULD BE LOTS OF RUBBER LEFT AND AT LEAST 1MM ($\frac{1}{25}$IN) BETWEEN THE PAD AND THE RIM OF THE WHEEL
- CHECK THE HEADSET FOR SMOOTH STEERING MOVEMENT, PAYING PARTICULAR ATTENTION TO ANY MOVEMENT BETWEEN THE FORKS AND THE FRAME. ANY PROBLEMS AND YOUR BIKE COULD BE DIFFICULT TO CONTROL
- HOLD ONE PEDAL STILL AND TRY TO MOVE THE OTHER ONE. IF THERE'S ANY MOVEMENT, YOU SHOULD TIGHTEN THE BOLTS

MONTHLY:
- CHECK THE LUBRICATION ON THE BRAKES, HUBS, GEARS AND BEARINGS (DEVICES DESIGNED TO MINIMISE FRICTION OF MOTION BETWEEN FIXED AND MOVING BIKE PARTS). AS YOU MAY HAVE GATHERED BY NOW, THERE ARE A LOT OF MOVING PARTS ON A BICYCLE, AND A DROP OF OIL WILL GO A LONG WAY TO KEEP THEM MOVING SMOOTHLY
- TIGHTEN ALL VISIBLE NUTS AND BOLTS ON YOUR RACKS, BRAKE LEVERS AND GEAR SHIFTERS
- CHECK FOR ANY FRAYING BRAKE AND GEAR CABLES
- GIVE YOUR BIKE A PROPER CLEAN USING LUBES AND DEGREASERS, BRUSHES AND SPONGES

Got a Problem With Your Wheels?

A helping hand

 PRACTICAL HINTS AND GUIDANCE FOR YOUR CAR.

 TOP ADVICE AND INFORMATION FOR YOUR MOTORCYCLE.

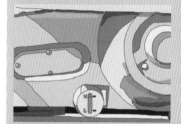

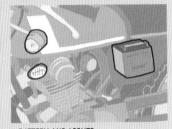

4 Wheels

Boot:
Used for storage. This should contain the spare wheel.

Fuel filler cap:
Unlock this to pour in the petrol or diesel.

Rear light cluster:
Includes rear, brake, reversing, indicator and fog lights.

Doors:
An odd number of doors (three or five) indicates a hatchback.

'The best car safety device is a rear-view mirror with a cop in it.'
DUDLEY MOORE

Wheels:
Usually include hubcaps unless the wheels are alloy.

Tyres:
Remember to rotate them every couple of years.

Front light cluster:
Includes headlights, sidelights and indicators.

Bonnet:
Under here is the engine (except on old VW Beetles, old Fiats and some sports cars).

What Car Should I Buy?

Women, eh? Can only distinguish cars by their colour? Before you decide on whether you want diesel or petrol, automatic or manual, you'll need to choose a body type. This means taking into account the amount of passengers or storage space you want as well as your lifestyle. So prove the cynics (and yourself) wrong by swatting up on the following . . .

A CRASH COURSE IN CARS

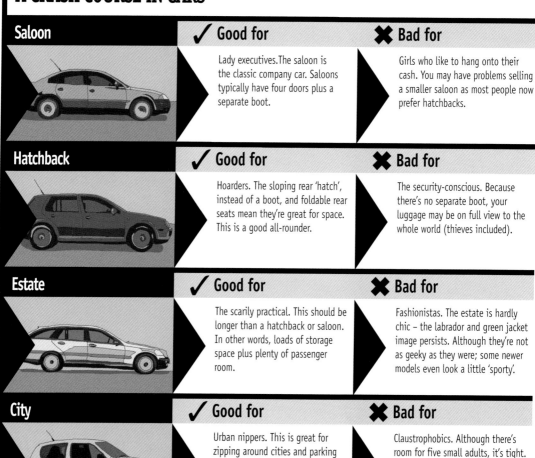

Saloon

✓ Good for
Lady executives. The saloon is the classic company car. Saloons typically have four doors plus a separate boot.

✗ Bad for
Girls who like to hang onto their cash. You may have problems selling a smaller saloon as most people now prefer hatchbacks.

Hatchback

✓ Good for
Hoarders. The sloping rear 'hatch', instead of a boot, and foldable rear seats mean they're great for space. This is a good all-rounder.

✗ Bad for
The security-conscious. Because there's no separate boot, your luggage may be on full view to the whole world (thieves included).

Estate

✓ Good for
The scarily practical. This should be longer than a hatchback or saloon. In other words, loads of storage space plus plenty of passenger room.

✗ Bad for
Fashionistas. The estate is hardly chic – the labrador and green jacket image persists. Although they're not as geeky as they were; some newer models even look a little 'sporty'.

City

✓ Good for
Urban nippers. This is great for zipping around cities and parking in teeny spaces.

✗ Bad for
Claustrophobics. Although there's room for five small adults, it's tight. And carrying bulky loads could prove problematic.

A CRASH COURSE IN CARS

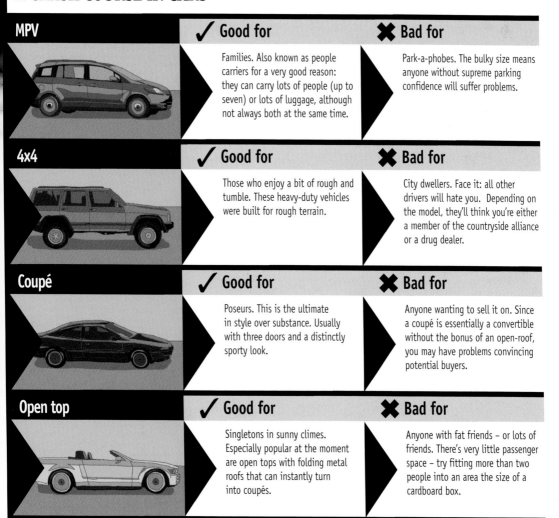

MPV

✓ **Good for**

Families. Also known as people carriers for a very good reason: they can carry lots of people (up to seven) or lots of luggage, although not always both at the same time.

✗ **Bad for**

Park-a-phobes. The bulky size means anyone without supreme parking confidence will suffer problems.

4x4

✓ **Good for**

Those who enjoy a bit of rough and tumble. These heavy-duty vehicles were built for rough terrain.

✗ **Bad for**

City dwellers. Face it: all other drivers will hate you. Depending on the model, they'll think you're either a member of the countryside alliance or a drug dealer.

Coupé

✓ **Good for**

Poseurs. This is the ultimate in style over substance. Usually with three doors and a distinctly sporty look.

✗ **Bad for**

Anyone wanting to sell it on. Since a coupé is essentially a convertible without the bonus of an open-roof, you may have problems convincing potential buyers.

Open top

✓ **Good for**

Singletons in sunny climes. Especially popular at the moment are open tops with folding metal roofs that can instantly turn into coupés.

✗ **Bad for**

Anyone with fat friends – or lots of friends. There's very little passenger space – try fitting more than two people into an area the size of a cardboard box.

| 4 Wheels | 2 Wheels | Pedal Power |

Know Your Car

Exterior

Before picking up a spanking new monkey wrench and donning a chic set of overalls, you'll need to know a little more about what's going on outside your car. It may look pretty straightforward, but confusing your hubcap with your petrol cap will damage your car as well as your pride.

1 **WINDSCREEN:** The windscreen must be scratch-free and squeaky clean. A scratch, however, does not necessarily mean a brand new windscreen. Try polishing it with glass polish or toothpaste (yes, really). Otherwise take to a windscreen repair specialist and see what they can do. Don't neglect your wipers either – they must be clean, grit-free and replaced when too worn.

2 **REAR LIGHT CLUSTER:** This includes an impressive five lights: rear, brake, reversing, indicator and fog. In some countries in Europe it is a legal requirement to carry spare bulbs. Even if it's not, carrying spare bulbs in the boot or glove compartment is a good idea.

3 **PETROL CAP:** The other big decision is petrol or diesel, both of which enter the car through this device. Choosing your fuel will affect your vehicle's performance: petrol is most common and petrol-run cars are generally cheaper to buy, but diesel, with its low CO_2, is fast catching on and gives more kilometres per litre (km/l) (miles per gallon (MPG)).

4 **WHEELS AND TYRES:** One aspect of choosing a car is deciding on front- or rear-wheel drive. In front-wheel drive cars, the entire drive chain is in the front, leaving more room for passengers and luggage. They also offer better handling in wet conditions. Basically, the front wheels pull the car along. In rear-wheel drive, the rear wheels push the car along.

5 **FRONT LIGHT CLUSTER:** This combines the headlights, sidelights and indicator lights. They must all be working correctly at all times. Pay special attention to your indicators, which should flash between one and two times per second.

First, though, a note on security. Since your car is an investment (see right) and could very well be the most expensive item you own, you don't want to lose it. One solution is choosing a car with a state-of-the-art security system. Deadlocks, for instance, stop the doors from being opened even if a window has been smashed, while an electronic immobiliser will prevent the engine from working. Thieves, quite frankly, don't stand a chance.

Yes, the dreaded D-word (that's 'depreciation' for anyone who's never tried reselling a car) is the bane of many a car-owner. As well as keeping your vehicle in tip-top condition for your own safety, you should also think about the future – after all, a car is a massive investment and, like any investment, you don't want to squander it.

- Make sure your car is regularly serviced and cleaned, both inside and out. Always retouch damaged paintwork immediately before it turns to rust.

- Mileage also counts towards depreciation. Don't expect to get top whack for your car if you've spent your time rallying round the globe.

- Buy a car – and a colour – that is already popular, especially one that is a good-buy second-hand. Certain reliable makes will fly off the used-car lot.

- Don't overdo the accessories: amazing speakers or fabulously plush leather seats will not only look out of place in a £3,000-banger, they won't help resell it.

- Most cars are worth considerably less than their new cost after their first year – and less than half after three years. If price bothers you, simply buy a used car.

- Don't smoke. The legend – 'Female driver, non-smoker' – is rooted in truth. That's exactly the sort of previous owner a prospective buyer wants!

Know Your Car

Interior

And now a peek inside. This is where all the action is – and as a driver this space will become your second home, or rather your second living room. If you've passed your test, you should be familiar with the various pedals and gearstick. But do you know the location of your bonnet-opening lever (crucial if you need to check the engine)? Thought not . . .

Steering wheel and horn

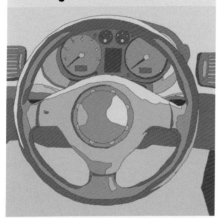

When you have both hands on the top of the wheel, there should be a slight bend in your elbows. If not, adjust the position of your seat. The indicators will be on either the left or the right of the wheel. The horn – sometimes in the centre of the wheel, sometimes on the indicator stalk – must always be working correctly. Some flashy cars may have an automatic gear-changing system attached to the wheel developed from Formula 1 technology, while others may include a device that enables you to change the stereo volume and settings without moving your hands from the wheel. In the event of a crash, an airbag (if fitted in your car) should stop you from hitting the wheel.

Foot pedals

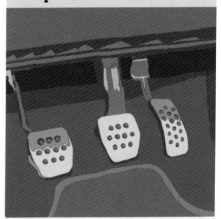

These make the car move and stop. To the right is the accelerator; this controls the speed of the car. Then there's the foot brake; touch this and your rear brake lights come on. The final pedal is the clutch, used when you move the car away, change gear and apply the brake. Some cars include cruise control: this means you can flick a switch and stop using the pedals altogether (although generally only on motorways). Automatics have no clutch pedal, but often have very large brake pedals, which can cover the equivalent space of the brake and clutch pedals on a manual. The bonnet-opening lever is often to be found in this area, but consult your car handbook for its exact location.

First, though, a quick reminder on the importance of interior cleaning – well, you want to keep everything in full working order and your car from depreciating, don't you? The seats should be vacuumed regularly, the floors swept and the dashboard and armrests wiped with a cleanser and damp chamois leather.

For more on cleaning, flip to pages 40–41. We did warn you it was like a living room.

Gearstick

Whether your car is an automatic or a manual, you'll still have a gearstick. This controls the gears, which in turn control the speed of the car in relation to the terrain and weather. However, the position of the stick can vary. Some older cars, for instance, have the gearstick mounted on the steering column (in essentially the same position as a huge indicator), while others have it situated on the dashboard.

Handbrake

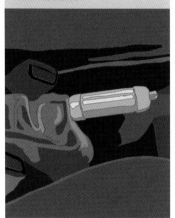

Necessary for emergency stops and to prevent your parked vehicle from sliding down a hill. A properly adjusted handbrake should click four to five times from being fully off before reaching the 'on' position. And again, there can be variations on the handbrake position. Some cars, for instance, have a handbrake situated in the footwell near to the driving pedals, creating a footbrake that serves the same purpose as a handbrake. Confusing stuff!

Seat mechanism

Necessary for adjusting the seat. Cars generally have one lever to alter the forward/backward position, and another to alter the reclining position. Some cars also have levers to adjust the height. A very posh car could include a computer-controlled seating system, which cleverly recognises your preferred position and changes it accordingly. Note that an incorrectly positioned seat – in other words, one where you can't easily reach the foot pedals – could result in loss of control.

Basic Car Kit

A handful of shopping bags in your boot will be no use whatsoever if you break down. What you really need to be carrying, boring as it may seem, is a tool kit. And no, the spare tyre and jack supplied with your car aren't sufficient. The following items – plus some know-how (which is why you've got this book) – will help release your inner Penelope Pitstop to fix most minor car troubles. Think of the kit as your makeup bag: some items are essential (mascara, lipstick), some not so necessary (eyelash curlers). Likewise, you can go overboard with car accessories – after all, you don't want to put those nice men in the AA out of business.

PRESSURE GAUGE	PLIERS	SCREWDRIVERS	SPANNERS	WHEEL BRACE	CLEAN CLOTH

Ideally, keep this in your glove compartment – gauges in garages aren't that accurate.	The tweezers of the tool world have a million and one uses.	Make sure to have a set that includes a flathead and a Phillips.	Buy a Russian Doll set, covering a range from 10–19mm.	Best to get one that has an extending handle – essential for removing nuts!	It gets dirty so that you don't have to.

For the super-cautious

Striking a balance between taking up too much space and having the necessary equipment to get you out of trouble is a tricky thing. If you're of a nervous disposition then the following will also come in handy.

Windscreen de-icer spray and scraper
If it's icy you'll be glad that you remembered this double act.

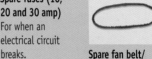
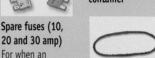

Spare fuses (10, 20 and 30 amp)
For when an electrical circuit breaks.

Can of WD40
Helpful when there's a wet, muggy atmosphere outside. Conditions such as fog can make the engine go damp; a quick spritz of this will kick-start it back into action.

Funnel

Engine oil
Make sure it's the right grade for your engine.

Windscreen washer fluid with additive

Empty petrol container

Spare fan belt/ drivebelt
In an emergency, a pair of tights might just do the trick (see page 37).

Tow rope/chain

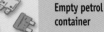

Travel rugs

Touch-up paint
To instantly go over any stone chippings before the damage gets rusty.

INSULATING TAPE

May well come in handy if there is a loose electrical connection.

FIRE EXTINGUISHER

Keep this handy under one of the seats, as when it comes to tackling a fire speed is the essence.

WARNING TRIANGLE

Obligatory if travelling in mainland Europe. Put it at least 50m (152ft) behind your car.

SPARE BULBS

This is regarded as compulsory on the Continent, and, at any rate, a good idea.

FIRST AID KIT

Always carry a first aid kit and remember that it is compulsory in parts of mainland Europe.

MOBILE PHONE

Official motoring bodies often recommend that all women drivers should carry a mobile phone.

CAR HANDBOOK

You'd be surprised at the number of people who leave this at home. Where it's of no use whatsoever.

TORCH

If there's a problem with your car, odds on it'll be dark and you'll have to peer under the bonnet.

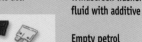

Tool Box Essentials

A surgeon without his instruments is useless. Likewise, a mechanic – however amateur – needs the correct kit. Before getting dirty, invest in the tools illustrated on the facing page since the ones supplied with your car will not be sufficient. Pack as much as you can in your boot – breakdowns have a nasty habit of being utterly unexpected – and store the remainder in your garage for the basic home maintenance you're about to learn.

 Greasy Gloria

Looking after the motor

Remember to keep your car in good nick. That means cleaning the windows and body regularly, and touching up scratches as soon as they appear.

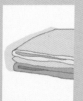 

Clean cloths: Have a few to hand so you don't get too grubby. Use old newspaper to mop up any big spills.

Windscreen washer fluid: Your washers must always have enough fluid, or you'll be left high and dry.

Cleansers and waxes: Gear necessary for cleaning and servicing (see pages 40–41 for more details).

Touch-up paint: Keep this handy to immediately paint over a scratch before any rust sets in.

Before you start tinkering, bear in mind the following Rules for Tools:

Rule one: invest in the best

As with most things in life, you get what you pay for. When choosing your tools, buy the best you can afford. Cheap tools have a short lifespan and could even damage your vehicle. If you buy a top-quality kit, it really will last you a lifetime.

If you're restricted to a tight budget, however, spend top whack on the tools that you're likely to use the most, namely a good set of screwdrivers, some pliers and an adjustable spanner.

Rule two: treat tools with TLC

No, the TLC isn't OTT. Don't leave your tools hanging around; instead keep them stored neatly together in a tool box. Ensure they are always clean and never, ever leave them wet – they'll only get rusty. And therefore useless.

If you leave your tools unused for any length of time, cover the metal parts with a thin layer of oil or grease. This will ensure that they will stay as fresh as the day you bought them.

Rule three: be gentle, please

Your car may be pretty hardcore but it's hardly a tank, so learn to use your tools correctly or you could end up damaging your motor for good. Spanners, for instance, should always be turned towards you as this gives you more control.

Another tip is to never over-tighten nuts and bolts. If you're unsure of your own strength, buy a torque wrench, a smart tool that makes a loud clicking sound when the correct amount of force has been applied.

A light touch is again necessary for any hammer work. Small dents, for example, can be lightly tapped out using a hammer covered in a cloth. But if you think you may be too heavy-handed, leave this job to the professionals.

Screwdrivers should be used for just that purpose – driving in screws – and not as general-purpose levers and chisels. This will only wreck the head of the screwdriver and bend the body out of shape.

Rule four: don't be a dirty girl

Car maintenance can get messy. Whether you're under the bonnet or changing a tyre, wear an outfit you don't mind ruining (overalls are best). Have heaps of clean rags and sheets of newspaper handy, remove any jewellery and protect your hands with plastic gloves – surgical gloves, available from most chemists, are ideal.

You're now ready to go. Good luck!

Box of delights

AMATEUR MECHANICS SHOULD MAKE SURE THEY HAVE ACCESS TO ALL THE TOOLS BELOW AND STORE THEM ALL TOGETHER IN A STURDY TOOL BOX IN THE GARAGE.

JACK: Lifts the car up so you can then change the wheel.

TORQUE WRENCH: This will make a loud click when the exact amount of force required for the nut and bolt has been applied. Very clever.

WHEEL BRACE: Vital if you need to get a wheel off.

SCREWDRIVERS: At least one of each type is necessary.

SPANNERS: Having a 10–19mm set in your tool box should cover your needs.

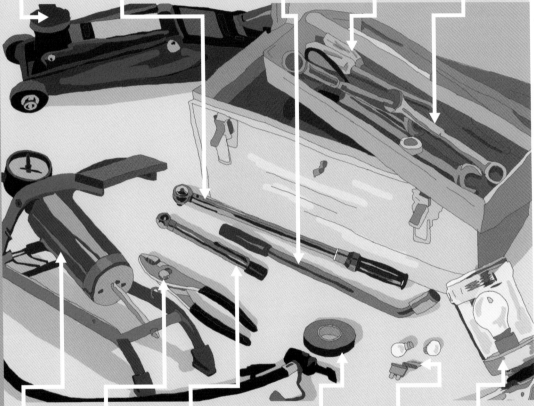

TYRE PUMP: To inflate your tyres (including your spare) when they get too low.

PLIERS: Always useful for tightening and undoing various components.

TYRE PRESSURE GAUGE: Vital for checking that your tyre pressures, including your spare, are correct – look in your car handbook for the exact measurements

INSULATING TAPE: Crucial for patching up any electrical circuits that may need repairing.

SPARE BULBS AND FUSES: You never know when your bulbs might pop. 10-, 20- and 30-amp fuses will sort a broken circuit.

TORCH: Perfect for those hard-to-see problem areas.

Understanding Your Dashboard and Controls

Be honest, now: when a red light starts flashing, is your first instinct, 'Argh! My vehicle is about to self-destruct'? To the uninitiated, the dashboard of a modern car can look like the control panel of a NASA shuttle – all that blinking and flashing and whirring of dials. But everything on your dashboard relates to what's going on in places you can't see. So once you know what's what, it's really very simple.

1 **INDICATOR SIGNALS:** Light up when each indicator is switched on.

2 **GLOWPLUG:** Only on cars with diesel engines, you must wait until the light is out before starting up.

3 **SAFETY BELTS:** Indicates whether or not your seat belt is fastened. It should be – it's the law.

4 **TACHOMETER:** This measures the engine speed in revs (revolutions) per minute (RPM).

5 **SPEEDOMETER:** Registers your car's speed.

6 **AIRBAG WARNING:** Lights up when there's a problem with the airbag system (if the car has one).

7 **LOW FUEL:** This will glow when fuel is low – fill it up IMMEDIATELY.

8 **FUEL GAUGE:** This will tell you how much fuel is left in your tank. You should visit a petrol station soon after it slips below halfway.

9 **TRIP METER:** Similar to an odometer, but can be reset so that the distance of individual journeys can be recorded.

10 **ODOMETER:** Counts the number of kilometres/miles your car has been driven.

11 **TEMPERATURE GAUGE:** This monitors the heat of the engine coolant. The arrow should rise slowly as you start the engine up from cold. It if moves into the red zone, your engine could be over-heating. Let the engine cool, and then check the level.

12 **BATTERY:** The warning light may mean the battery needs to be charged or the alternator (which converts the engine power into electricity) is faulty.

13 **OIL PRESSURE:** If this stays on, your oil could be low. Stop the engine and check the level.

14 **CHECK ENGINE:** This will light up when there is a problem with something not covered by the other warning lights. Stop the car and look under the bonnet.

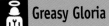

Greasy Gloria

If the arrow on your temperature gauge is in the hot zone, your engine may need to be cooled down. To do this: put the heater on high, which in turn transfers the heat from the engine into the car. However, this is only a temporary solution. Make a visual check under the bonnet for coolant leaks and seek professional advice if the problem persists.

15 DOORS OPEN: Lights up when one or more of the doors has not been fully closed.

16 HIGH-BEAM HEADLIGHTS: Use these at night only when there's no oncoming traffic.

17 BRAKING SYSTEM: If this glows then your brake fluid level is low. Don't drive the car until you have rectified the problem. It could also mean that your handbrake is on, or that your brake pads need changing.

If it's the latter, have the pads renewed as quickly as possible.

18 HAZARD LIGHTS: Shows that the hazard warning lights (which are actually both indicators flashing simultaneously) are on. This can sometimes be a button itself, which activates the lights when pressed. Use only in an emergency.

Car Science: Understanding Your Vehicle's Engine

Before you even begin to tackle the most basic car maintenance, you need to know what goes on under the bonnet. To the uninitiated – that means you – what lurks beneath the bonnet may on first impressions appear an unknown, shady world, a world that necessitates the amount of passion and knowledge only shared by men. You need to banish those thoughts immediately. Open the bonnet and, with the help of this page, acquaint yourself with the various parts. Believe it or not, understanding how the engine works doesn't require a degree in mechanics or an enlarged left side of brain. After all, if men can do it, so can you!

Engine and fuel-injection

What is the engine's basic function?

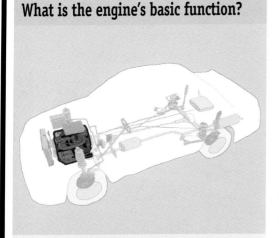

That's simple: to burn fuel to produce the power that drives the vehicle. The fuel depends on the type of car but is most probably either petrol or diesel.

And the engine's basic components?
Engines are primarily made up of cylinders. Most cars have four, but some have up to 12. Fuel goes via the fuel-injection system or carburettor into the cylinder through a valve, and leaves through another valve out into the exhaust system. It is inside the cylinder that the fuel is burned. The resulting explosion pushes the pistons down to produce power.

And what is the fuel-injection system?

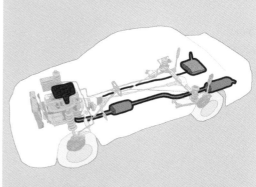

The fuel-injection system delivers fuel into the cylinder head. Travelling from the tank, the fuel goes down the fuel line, via the fuel filter (which removes any impurities), via the fuel-injection system (or carburettor) to the engine block.

Is it simply fuel, then?
No, this is where the fuel-injection system comes into play. The fuel is always mixed with air before it enters the cylinder. This air is passed through an air filter and mixes with the fuel in the fuel-injection system (or carburettor on older vehicles).

Ignition and oil

What happens when I turn the key?

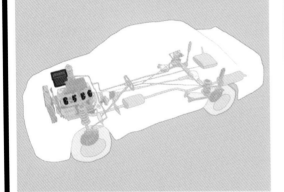

Turning the ignition key starts a chain of events that eventually creates an electrical spark, which ignites the fuel/air mixture in the engine's cylinder (on diesel engines this mixture ignites itself). This results in a tiny explosion that pushes the cylinder's piston down. This in turn moves the crankshaft, which converts the up-and-down motion into rotational motion – all the crankshafts are connected with rods so the resulting action works like bicycle pedals. Then, thanks to the transmission (essentially a cluster of spinning gears next to the engine block) this pedal-action rotates the wheels. The gears control the amount of power necessary from the engine to the wheels. You can now move away!

What about the oil?

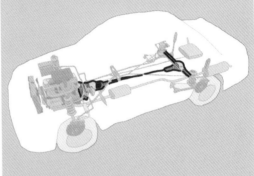

The oil plays no part in the engine combustion process. Instead it serves to lubricate the moving parts of the engine, in particular the pistons and crankshaft. It also keeps the engine cool, as indeed does the coolant (a mixture of water and anti-freeze). It is therefore crucial that you always use the correct grade of oil and keep it at the right level, otherwise engine parts will wear out rapidly and expensively.

Basic Maintenance and Repairs

First, a few safety measures. If you have long hair, tie it back. Also remove any jewellery – you don't want your dangly earrings getting stuck in the fan belt. Put on some overalls and a pair of plastic gloves. Keep the garage door open for ventilation. Oh, and don't smoke – you don't want your car turning into a mini bomb. The following Chore Chart is based on the assumption that you drive daily. Follow the instructions religiously and not only will you save money on repair bills, you will also reduce some of the depreciation that is inevitable when it comes to reselling the car.

Chore Chart: What to do when

 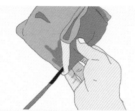 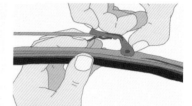

DAILY:

- INSPECT FOR FLAT TYRES
- WALK AROUND THE CAR AND ENSURE NOTHING IS DAMAGED, PAYING SPECIAL ATTENTION TO BOTH FRONT AND REAR LIGHTS
- CHECK THE LIGHTS AND INDICATORS ARE WORKING CORRECTLY
- MAKE SURE WINDSCREENS AND WINDOWS ARE CLEAN
- TEST THE BRAKES WORK BY SQUEEZING THE PEDAL SHORTLY AFTER DRIVING OFF

WEEKLY:

- CHECK THE FUEL LEVEL – THIS SHOULD ALWAYS BE ABOVE THE HALFWAY MARK – AND LOOK FOR ANY LEAKS
- INSPECT THE OIL; AGAIN, THIS SHOULD BE ABOVE THE HALFWAY MARK ON THE DIPSTICK. ALSO LOOK FOR LEAKS
- CHECK THE BRAKE AND CLUTCH FLUID AND LOOK FOR LEAKS
- EXAMINE THE COOLANT LEVEL IN THE RADIATOR – THIS SHOULD BE DONE WHEN THE ENGINE IS COLD. AND AGAIN, LOOK FOR LEAKS
- MAKE SURE THERE'S SUFFICIENT FLUID IN THE WINDSCREEN WASHER RESERVOIR
- ASK SOMEONE TO HELP YOU CHECK THE BRAKE LIGHTS
- CHECK THE BATTERY CONNECTIONS ARE TIGHT AND CLEAN AND TOP UP WITH DISTILLED WATER – NEVER TAP – IF NECESSARY (YOU WON'T HAVE TO DO THIS IF THE BATTERY IS SEALED)

MONTHLY:

- TEST YOUR TYRES' PRESSURE WHEN THEY ARE COLD – AND DON'T FORGET THE SPARE. ALSO CHECK THE TYRE TREAD
- MAKE SURE THE FAN BELT IS SUFFICIENTLY TIGHT AND IS NOT WORN
- CHECK THE WIPER BLADES. REPLACE IF WORN
- GIVE THE CAR A THOROUGH CLEAN AND POLISH
- IF YOU NORMALLY ONLY USE THE CAR FOR SHORT TRIPS, TAKE IT OUT ON A LONGER RUN. THIS IS GOOD FOR THE ENGINE AND RECHARGES THE BATTERY

EVERY SIX MONTHS OR SO:

- CHECK COMPONENTS – AIR FILTER, FUEL FILTER AND SPARK PLUGS SHOULD BE CHANGED AT THE SERVICE INTERVALS RECOMMENDED IN YOUR HANDBOOK. THIS SHOULD BE CARRIED OUT WHEN YOU TAKE YOUR CAR IN FOR ITS SERVICE

Greasy Gloria's No-Nos

1. Don't leave the fuel tank less than half full

This might sound overly cautious, but you should always leave the tank at least half full. If it starts running dry, the sediment from the tank could end up in the fuel system. This in turn could cause the engine to stall and lead to more serious problems. A half-empty tank will also attract water vapour. And another fuel point: don't keep changing the grade as this will only confuse your engine. Stick to what the handbook recommends.

2. Don't forget your car's other fluids

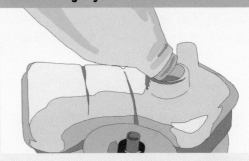

This means the oil, brake fluid, clutch fluid and coolant. You should check their levels weekly and also inspect for any leaks. If you neglect the oil, for instance, you could end up damaging your engine and spending a fortune on repairs. Similarly, getting amnesia over the coolant in your radiator could result in your engine overheating. A five-minute check should mean stress-free driving.

3. Don't leave your battery to rot

Any repairs to your car's electrical system should really be left to the professionals. But this doesn't mean you can forget it altogether as a faulty battery is a prime cause of breakdowns. First switch off the engine. Then check the outside of the battery for any damage and make sure the cables aren't fraying. Most batteries are maintenance-free. Some, however, require regular inspection of the electrolyte level – you may need to top this up with distilled water. If a white, powdery deposit has formed on the terminals, pour hot water over them and then coat with Vaseline.

4. Don't overlook your tyres

These are your only contact with the road, so treat them with the respect they deserve. Good tread is necessary for difficult weather conditions and road surfaces; if the tread reaches 1.6mm (¹⁄₁₆in) it's too worn and the tyre should be replaced immediately. As for the pressure, look in your car handbook to find out the correct level for your vehicle and the type of tyres fitted. Under-inflated tyres damage more quickly. They also increase your vehicle's overall fuel consumption. Over-inflated tyres wear more rapidly. Costly either way.

Under Pressure

Always buy the right tyres for your make of car and for your driving conditions – and always aim for the best ones you can afford. For tyre maintenance, you'll need two distinct tools: a tread gauge and a tyre pressure gauge. It's worth investing in your own since pressure gauges at petrol stations can be wildly inaccurate. And in theory you can use a coin to inspect the tread, but that, too, is likely to be way off the mark.

CHECKING YOUR TYRE PRESSURE

Having the correct pressure is of the utmost importance – both under- and over-inflated tyres wear much more quickly. Tyre pressure can decrease as the temperature drops, so check regularly, especially during the winter months.

1 Check the pressure when the tyres are cold (this means they haven't been driven for at least 30 minutes). If they're still warm, you could get a misleading reading.

2 The pressure is measured in metric bars or pounds per square inch (psi). The correct pressure for your car can be found in its manual. The front and rear tyres often have different settings.

3 Remove the cap from the valve stem.

4 Press the rounded end of the gauge against the valve stem. Make sure no air escapes.

5 Remove the gauge.

6 Read the measurement using the ruler end of the gauge.

7 Repeat with all four tyres.

8 Oh, and don't forget the spare!

Greasy Gloria

Even the most box-fresh of tyres will have some irregularities. The solution? Get your tyres balanced regularly to stop any wobbling. This is another job for the mechanic – don't ever attempt this at home.

If the tyre pressure is too high:

Gently press the pin in the centre of the tyre valve to release air. Do a little at a time.

And if it is too low:

Visit your nearest petrol station as soon as possible for more air from the compressed air machine, or if you have your own pump, use that.

CHECKING YOUR TYRE TREAD

Good tread is necessary for difficult weather conditions and road surfaces; if the tread reaches 1.6mm ($\frac{1}{15}$in) it's too worn and the tyre should be replaced immediately. You should check each tyre at two different points. While checking your tyre tread, also look for signs of wear.

Another top tip is rotating your tyres to even out tread wear – in other words, replacing the two front ones with the rear ones periodically. Ask a mechanic to do this and include the spare tyre in the rotation, unless it's a compact spare.

If the tread is worn out more on one side, this could mean that the tyres need to be aligned. A visit to a mechanic or tyre specialist should sort this out.

Wheel Love

Oh, my. There are some things in life you just can't predict and, even though it's a very common problem, getting a flat is one of them. But you can prepare yourself. However boring it may sound, novices should practise changing a wheel and using a jack at home. You never know when you'll need it.

CHANGING A WHEEL

1 First, make sure your car is parked on a level surface. Put on the handbrake and put the car into first gear (if it's an automatic, move to 'P'). If stranded on a road, put your warning triangle at least 50m (152ft) behind the vehicle.

2 Chock the wheel diagonally opposite the one that needs to be changed with wooden blocks, bricks or large stones. If you're carrying nothing suitable, be inventive.

3 If there's a hubcap, remove it. Using the wheel brace, slacken each bolt on the affected wheel. Do this in a crisscross pattern: loosen one bolt, then the one opposite, and so forth.

4 Fit the jack into the jacking point (often a small notch under the frame) closest to the affected wheel. Slide the spare wheel under the car near the wheel that's about to be removed, but away from the jack. Raise the jack until the wheel is off the ground.

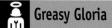
Greasy Gloria

If you've just had a new tyre fitted, check that Popeye hasn't tightened the bolts. Try slackening and then tightening them before setting out for the first time. Otherwise, if you do ever get a flat, you might not be able to remove the wheel, let alone change it.

5 Remove the bolts and lift off the wheel.

6 Put the spare wheel into place, then refit and tighten the bolts; first with your fingers, again in a crisscross pattern. Remove the faulty wheel, lower the jack and remove that from the car.

7 With the wheel brace, fully tighten the bolts in a crisscross pattern. Replace the hubcap. And you can now drive off into the sunset!

8 BUT if using a compact spare (a temporary spare tyre), don't drive any faster than 80km/h (50mph) and get it replaced as soon as possible.

Liquid News

Your car needs a surprising amount of juice to keep it running smoothly – namely oil, coolant, brake fluid, hydraulic clutch fluid and maybe even power steering fluid. All these fluids need their levels checking regularly, and all need to be inspected for leaks.

OIL

If your engine doesn't have the correct amount of oil – in the right grade – it could end up seriously damaged. Check with your car handbook for the type of oil that's right for your car. To check your oil . . .

1 Make sure the engine is cold and that the car is on a level surface.

2 The instrument used to check the oil is called the dipstick. Pull it out and wipe it with a clean cloth. Return it fully, pull out again and check the oil mark.

3 Try not to let the oil level slip below halfway; likewise, it shouldn't be over-full.

To fill up:

1 Find the oil filler cap (it's usually marked 'oil').

2 Unscrew it and pour in a small quantity of oil – a funnel may help.

3 Wait a few seconds and then recheck the level with the dipstick.

4 Wipe off any oil you may have spilled.

5 Refit the filler cap – make sure it's tight – and ensure that the dipstick is pushed fully back into its tube.

6 A final tip: never over-fill the engine with oil as this could cause leaks. This is why you should fill it little by little.

COOLANT

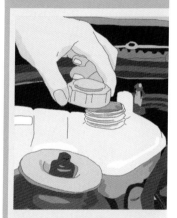

Coolant is a mixture of one-third anti-freeze and two-thirds water. This stops your engine from getting too hot (and from freezing) and also prevents rusting inside your radiator. Check your car's handbook to make sure you use the right type of coolant.

1 Park your car on level ground. Open the bonnet and look for a plastic container marked with 'Min' and 'Max' levels.

2 Check the level when the engine is cold. The level should be near the maximum point. If not, unscrew the cap and top it up with coolant.

3 Also check for leaks. If you have to fill up the container often (say, every two months), there might be a leak. Seek professional help.

POWER STEERING FLUID

Your car may also need power steering fluid, so check in the handbook whether there's a separate reservoir for this too. If so, top up with the appropriate fluid recommended by your manufacturer, using the same directions as suggested below under 'clutch fluid'.

BRAKE FLUID

If the brake fluid gets too low your brakes will work inefficiently – or not at all. Checking your brakes must be done as swiftly as possible because brakes don't like contact with air or any moisture.

1 Make sure the car is parked on level ground. Open the bonnet and locate the brake fluid reservoir – it should be located behind your engine.

2 Unscrew the cap and check the level. If it is below the 'Max' mark, top up. Always use fluid from a new container – exposure to air, however fleeting, contaminates it, so dispose of any remainder.

3 Also check the quality of the fluid by dipping a finger in and then rubbing the liquid between your hands. If it feels gritty, get a mechanic to change it.

4 As the brakes wear, the fluid level will drop – this is normal. But if you're topping up the levels on a regular basis, there may be a leak. Get this fixed immediately.

CLUTCH FLUID

For this, somewhat confusingly, you also use brake fluid – check with your car handbook for the correct grade. The clutch sometimes shares a common reservoir with the brake fluid; look in your car handbook for details. The clutch fluid ensures the smooth operation of the clutch when you change gears. If your vehicle has a mechanical clutch – as opposed to hydraulic – there will be no clutch fluid reservoir.

1 Park on level ground. Open your bonnet – the clutch fluid reservoir should be behind the engine.

2 The level should be between 'Min' and 'Max'.

3 If you need to top up, unscrew the cap and top up with new fluid – always use a freshly opened bottle. Again, dispose of the leftovers.

4 If there is a massive loss, there could be a leak. Seek professional advice immediately.

Fan Club

Remember those old 1950s films when a woman whips off her tights and ties them round some cogs under the bonnet? Well, she's using the tights as a makeshift fan belt. Often referred to nowadays as the drivebelt, this drives certain bits of the engine such as the air-conditioning compressor and the power steering. There may be one fan belt – or there may be several. You should always check your fan belt as part of your monthly maintenance plan (see page 28).

HOW TO CHECK THE FAN BELT

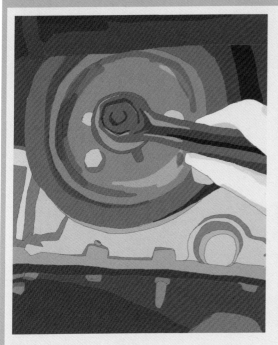

1 Firstly, always carry a spare fan belt. Make sure you buy the right type for your car – consult your car handbook for the correct one for your vehicle. If you can't fix it, then hopefully someone else can.

2 Open the bonnet and find the fan belt. This may require turning the engine. To do this: use a spanner on the bolt attached to the crankshaft and turn.

3 Look for any damage or fraying. Also watch out for any hard glazed patches. Any irregularities mean that the fan belt must be changed.

4 To replace the fan belt: loosen both the adjusting bolt and the alternator bolts. Move the alternator towards the engine cylinder block. Slip the old belt off and the new one on.

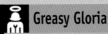
And back to ladies' tights. So can you use them as an impromptu fan belt? To be honest, it's doubtful – many claim this is merely an urban myth or a good way to set your car on fire. Play it safe, then, and always carry a spare fan belt with you when driving. If, however, you're really stuck, it might be worth giving the tights a try.

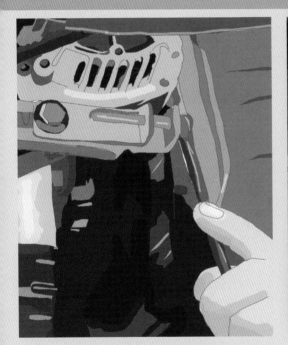

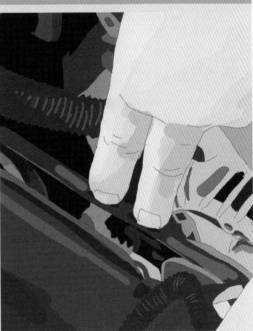

5 Make sure you fit the belt with the right tension. After a little practice, this shouldn't be too hard – it will squeal if it's too slack and hum if it's too tight. A good guide is if you can push the belt down with your finger by between 5–10mm (⅕–⅖in). You should be able to.

6 You can actually drive a little way with a broken fan belt although it depends what the affected belt was operating. Don't drive if it was the fan belt for the coolant pump, fuel injection pump or hydraulic pump.

7 But it's OK to drive with a broken alternator, power steering or air-conditioning fan belt. But you should only drive for a small distance before fixing the problem.

8 Of course, if you are in any doubt whatsoever, don't drive at all and call for assistance.

I Can See Clearly Now

Windscreens, believe it or not, are easy to overlook when it comes to car maintenance. The reckoning being that since the driver is staring out of it daily, any problems will be obvious. Wrong. Bet you haven't considered your wipers (blades that work properly are actually a legal requirement). Or, indeed, your washer reservoir . . .

WIPER BLADE MAINTENANCE

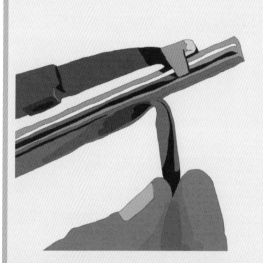

Don't wait until you're caught in a heavy storm with zero vision. New blades are cheap and easy to install.

1 Every now and then, check the blades for baldness – and don't forget your rear wiper blade. You need to make sure all blades are working efficiently.

2 Lift the arm from the screen, check the blade rubber and then wipe the edge of the blade with some windscreen washer fluid and a cloth.

3 Do the blades squeak? Do they smear? If so, you'll need to replace them with new ones. Make sure you buy the right blades for the make and model of your car.

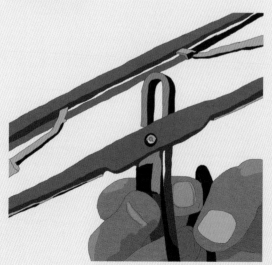

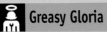
Consider carrying some windscreen washer fluid in your boot – you never know when you'll need it. And another tip: don't use a higher wiper speed than necessary when it's raining, as this will only make your blades wear down more quickly.

WASHER RESERVOIR MAINTENANCE

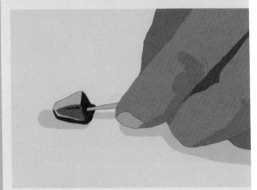

4 To fit new blades: first, turn the ignition off.

5 Lift up the wiper arm until it locks.

6 Remove the blade. Turn it at right angles to the wiper arm, then slide it out. Don't let the arm ping back.

7 Fit the new blade – check the packet for precise details – and then lower the arm back into position on the windscreen.

8 Check the wipers are working correctly before driving off.

9 During winter your blades may stick to the windscreen. You can free them using de-icer.

You should check this weekly as well.

1 Open the bonnet – yes, confusingly, the reservoir is under here. The rear wiper generally uses the same reservoir; if not, it will be in the boot.

2 The reservoir should be full. If it's not, fill up with washer fluid using a funnel. You can even buy specially formulated fluids for summer (fluid that can remove dead insects) and winter (fluid that won't freeze). If you do choose seasonal fluids, though, remember to swap them over when the seasons change.

3 Also check the nozzles. These spray the fluid onto the windscreen and can easily get clogged up. Clean away any gunk using something pointy like a needle and work it down the eye of the jet. At the same time make sure they are properly positioned. Reposition with your fingers.

Shampooing Your Car

Beauty isn't skin deep. When it comes to cars, a good cleanse, tone and moisturise routine will not only stop your vehicle from rusting away, it will also make it easier to resell. Keep your car buffed and beautiful and everything should be just peachy. After all, don't you want to look good on the road?

Cleaning kit

- CAR SHAMPOO
- SPONGE
- BUCKET
- HOSE
- PLENTY OF CLEAN CLOTHS
- BRUSH FOR THE TYRES
- WAX
- CHROME/METAL POLISH
- CHAMOIS LEATHER
- VACUUM CLEANER WITH SLIM HEAD
- VARIOUS CLEANERS FOR THE INTERIOR

WASHING AND WAXING

1 Wait until the car is cold. And don't clean your car in direct sunlight – the same goes for drying.

2 Start with the wheels. Spray the tyres; then clean with a brush and plenty of car shampoo and water.

3 Now concentrate on the body. Start at the roof and work down, cleaning with lots of shampoo and a sponge. Rinse thoroughly using the hose, all the while looking for any scratches or chips. Dry with a chamois leather.

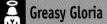 **Greasy Gloria**

Don't forget your windows . . .

Treat them like the windows of your house. Spritz with a glass cleaner (use one that's been specially formulated for a car), then wipe with a chamois leather. And don't forget your windscreen – it's not fair to leave your wipers with all the work. And don't smoke inside the car – this only makes the windows even dirtier.

4 Now it's time to wax – this will prevent rust. Don't do this in strong sunlight, either. Liquid waxes are easiest to use.

5 Put the wax on with one cloth, wipe off and buff with another. Work in one small area at a time.

6 Finally, polish the chrome and metal bits (such as handles) with a specially formulated polish.

CLEANING THE ENGINE

Use a clean cloth to wipe away any dirt and grease from the reservoirs, the radiator, under the bonnet and the battery. This will not only make the engine look good, but it will also help to keep it running smoothly.

DEALING WITH RUST, SCRATCHES AND DENTS

Any rust should be tackled the moment it's discovered. Scrape it with a wire brush and follow this with emery paper. Then use a special rust treatment, available from all good car shops. Finish with a dab of touch-up paint, which comes either in brush or aerosol form – make sure you get the exact shade.

If you find a scratch, clean round it with water, then paint over using the touch-up paint. Do this slowly and carefully in the same direction. Wait for a few days for everything to settle, then rub the area with a polishing compound to blend the new paint in.

A small dent can be lightly tapped out using a hammer covered in a cloth. But, as with all of the above, if you don't feel fully confident doing the job, leave it to the professionals. You could end up doing further damage to your car.

CLEANING THE INTERIOR

We've already compared the inside of your car to your living room – so treat it accordingly. Start with decluttering – remove any empty drink cans and sweet wrappers. Then vacuum the seats, paying special attention to the backs of the seats where crumbs like to gather. Remove any spills with a suitable stain remover. Move to the floor, remembering to remove the rubber mats. End with the details – the dashboard and armrests – using a cleanser compatible with the material. A wipe with the damp chamois may be sufficient here.

Troubleshooting Q&A

If your car won't start, it could be something as simple as there being no fuel in the tank. On the other hand, it could be something more serious. Use a methodical approach to diagnose the possible cause. If it's easy to solve, then fix it using this book. If not, then seek professional help immediately. Driving with a fault is simply not worth the risk.

Problem	Cause & Solution
✖ **Car won't start**	✔ **Fuel level or battery**
Hmmm, you've turned the key but can't get your car to start.	Is the fuel tank empty? Is the battery flat? If you're still having no joy, then there could be an electrical problem, so visit a mechanic.
✖ **Odd sound when starting up**	✔ **Starter motor or driveshaft**
When you start up the car, there's a funny whirring sound.	This could be down to a defective starter motor or a dodgy driveshaft. Both require professional assistance.
✖ **Battery light comes on**	✔ **Battery**
The battery light on the dashboard is glowing red while you are driving – it feels like a warning.	It is: your battery could be flat or your engine may not be working. Turn off the ignition, inspect the battery, then seek professional help.
✖ **Spongy brakes**	✔ **Brake fluid**
When you push the brake pedal it feels spongy. And not very safe.	Check the brake fluid – is it at the right level? Otherwise you could be experiencing trouble with your callipers or hoses, another job for a mechanic.
✖ **Hissing noise**	✔ **Radiator**
When you stop the car, you can hear a hissing sound from under the bonnet.	Open the bonnet – cautiously – and look at the radiator. Is there an obvious leak or fault? If not, it's off to the mechanic again.

Problem	Cause & Solution
✖ **Gears feel clunky**	✓ **Gearbox**
There's a clunky sound – and feeling – when you're changing gears.	Check the transmission fluid level. If the problem persists, you may need assistance. Don't leave this fault too long as it could get expensive.
✖ **Squeaky brakes**	✓ **Brake pads**
You squeeze the brake pedal to stop – and it squeaks.	Is this a new thing? Some brakes simply squeak. But if yours are usually as silent as a (non-squeaky) mouse, you may need new pads.
✖ **Liquid under car**	✓ **Fluids**
There's a puddle of liquid on the road under your car.	First identify the liquid. If it's water, don't worry – it's simply a by-product of your air conditioning. Anything else (oil, coolant or other fluid) means a leak, so consult a mechanic.
✖ **Car stalls**	✓ **Battery or air filter**
Your car stalls more often than it should in cold weather.	Check the air filter and the battery – both can cause your car to stall. Still no luck? Then call a mechanic.
✖ **Steering feels unsafe**	✓ **Tyres or wheels**
You're suddenly finding it very difficult to steer.	Your tyres should be the first place you look – check for flats and low pressure. Otherwise it could be your wheels, which will require professional assistance.

Ready, Steady . . . Go! The Ten-minute Road Check

On the road, you may feel less vulnerable than a motorcycle and less precarious than a bike, but that doesn't mean you're invincible. If you're thoughtless with your maintenance, you could harm yourself as well as others. So be good and do a quick run-through of the following pointers as often as possible – in an ideal world, this would be every time you set out or at the start of any long journey. Any problems, and turn back to the relevant page in this book for help.

1 **MIRRORS:** Check all mirrors are correctly positioned and look for any cracks.

2 **LIGHTS:** The headlights and rear lights, sidelights, brake lights, fog lights and indicators must all be working properly. Replace any dead bulbs immediately.

3 **FUEL:** The tank should be always at least half full. After all that hard work, you don't want to be caught short!

4 **WHEELS AND TYRES:** It's wise to do a visual check before every journey. Keep a lookout for any cuts and debris, and monitor the general wear and state of the tread. Make sure the tyres are inflated to the correct pressure. And don't forget the spare.

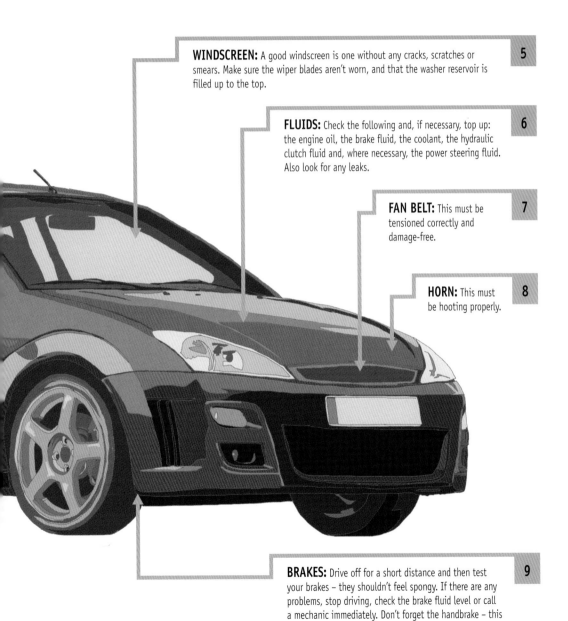

WINDSCREEN: A good windscreen is one without any cracks, scratches or smears. Make sure the wiper blades aren't worn, and that the washer reservoir is filled up to the top.

5

FLUIDS: Check the following and, if necessary, top up: the engine oil, the brake fluid, the coolant, the hydraulic clutch fluid and, where necessary, the power steering fluid. Also look for any leaks.

6

FAN BELT: This must be tensioned correctly and damage-free.

7

HORN: This must be hooting properly.

8

BRAKES: Drive off for a short distance and then test your brakes – they shouldn't feel spongy. If there are any problems, stop driving, check the brake fluid level or call a mechanic immediately. Don't forget the handbrake – this must also work perfectly at all times.

9

Carrying a Load

In the same way that you can't use an evening bag for work, sometimes a boot just isn't big enough for all your booty. Luckily, a few natty accessories will help you deal with heavy or bulky loads.

First of all, though, whatever the load, it's crucial that your visibility isn't blocked in any way. Also make sure that your headlights are adjusted as your suspension may be lower at the back. And remember to consider the cost – a heavy car will guzzle fuel.

In the boot:

If your load is so bulky that the boot won't close, tie it down with rope and make sure that the number plate and lights are still legally visible. Ensure the load is totally secure before setting off.

Tow business

THIS IS WHEN EXTRA LOADS GET REALLY BIG. TOWING SAFELY IS A SKILL, SO IT'S BEST TO GO ON A TRIAL RUN BEFORE EMBARKING ON A LONG JOURNEY AND PRACTISE ANY TRICKY MANOEUVRES SUCH AS REVERSING (DO THIS IN AN EMPTY CAR PARK IF YOU CAN). WITH A CARAVAN/TRAILER BEHIND YOU, IT'S ONE HUNDRED TIMES MORE COMPLICATED. SOME OTHER POINTS:

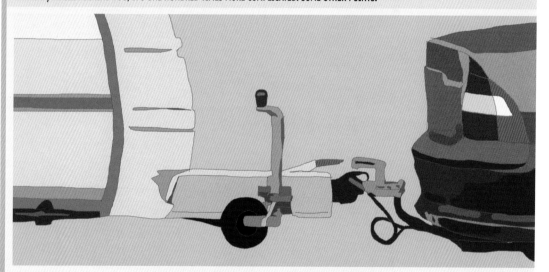

- You need a really good tow bar, the best you can afford. If possible, splash out on a professional installation.

- Make sure you even out the weight between the car and the trailer. Don't load everything into the trailer and leave your car empty.

- Think about lowering your speed and braking in good time. Your handling may also be affected, so never overlook your suspension. Basically, it all boils down to driving more carefully.

- Using your car's side mirrors, ensure you can see clearly behind the trailer/caravan. If necessary, buy extending mirrors.

- Check all your lights. Make sure the trailer/caravan lights are working. Also check to see if your headlights need adjusting.

The art of carrying a load

Roof rack

Some racks are specific to a particular make or model of car, but most are universal. Make sure yours is securely fitted. And whatever you do, don't exceed the maximum load weight specified in your car handbook.

When carrying a load, bear in mind that wind resistance can be bad. Wrap the load in tarpaulin, then tie it down with elastic cords. Check the load is secure before setting off.

Bike rack

Bike enthusiasts can carry their cycles on the roof or on a bike carrier attached to the rear of the car. If opting for the latter, remember that other road users must still be able to read your car number plate; you may need to buy an additional plate plus another set of lights.

Ski box

This hard-shelled box is designed especially for transporting skis. It is fixed atop a couple of roof rails running along either side of the car roof.

Top box

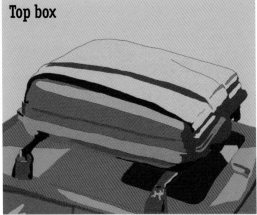

Similar in design to the ski box, the difference being that this can be used for a variety of luggage. Top boxes are aerodynamic – so wind resistance shouldn't be too much of a problem – and can also be locked.

Carrying Passengers: Driving With Children

Unless you are a confirmed singleton who will only ever drive a two-seater city car or a sporty soft-top, at some time in your life you'll probably end up driving with children. Since cars are designed with adult passengers in mind, children require special treatment. Adults in car crashes usually break their legs. Children, on the other hand, suffer much more serious injuries such as damage to the pelvis and ruptured spleens.

First of all, the law. In the UK, children under three years old must be fastened into the appropriate child restraint if carried in the front seat. Wherever possible, though, carry children in the back – it's safer there, plus airbags when activated can kill a young child. In fact, it's recommended that all children under 13 ride in the back seat. UK law also states that you must use an appropriate restraint if carrying your child in the back.

There are literally hundreds of baby/child seat options to choose from. Quite shockingly, most are installed incorrectly – so follow the manufacturer's instructions VERY carefully.

The art of carrying a load

Baby seat

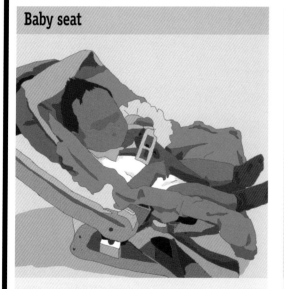

These are for babies, from new-borns to at least one-year-olds, and often convert into carriers when removed from the car.

Fasten the baby in first. Secure the harness, with the shoulder straps flat and at or below the baby's shoulders. There should be no slack, and blankets should go over the child. Fasten the seat securely to the middle of the back seat facing the rear – this is the safest spot. Follow the manufacturer's instructions carefully. The baby should recline at a 45-degree angle.

Child safety seat

These are aimed at toddlers. You should allow your child to face the rear for as long as possible – basically until he/she has outgrown the position – for optimum safety.

Graduate to facing forward. When your child moves onto a child seat, the shoulder straps should now be at or above shoulder level. The chest clips should be level with the armpits. Again, aim for the centre of the back seat and read the instructions properly. And remember, there must be no slack in the harness.

And when should a child move onto using just the seat belt?

Use the following pointers as a test:

- Can the child sit all the way back in the car seat?
- Do his/her knees bend around the edge of the seat in a comfortable way?
- Does the safety belt go across the shoulder between the neck and the arm?
- Does the lap belt touch the thighs?

If even one of the answers to the above questions is no, stick with the booster seat until your child has grown.

Booster seat

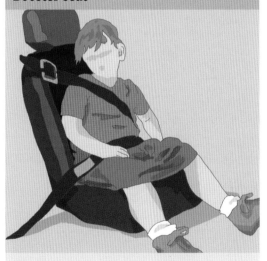

Booster seats are used after child safety seats and before the rite of passage that is using the car's actual seat belt. The child should be at least three years old. Make sure the shoulder and lap belts fit properly. If the child's ears rise above the top of the back seat, get a booster with a high back.

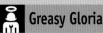

Animal farm

NEVER WORK WITH ANIMALS OR CHILDREN, SO THE OLD ADAGE GOES. THE SAME COULD APPLY TO DRIVING, BUT UNFORTUNATELY IT CAN'T ALWAYS BE AVOIDED. HOW YOU CARRY AN ANIMAL OF COURSE DEPENDS ON ITS SIZE. HERE ARE SOME BASIC GUIDELINES TO KEEP BOTH YOU AND YOUR PET SAFE.

- In a crash, not only could the pet get hurt, it could also hurt you. Unrestrained pets can also distract the driver – and hence cause a crash. Visit a reputable pet shop and ask for advice on the best seat belt harness, pet carrier or cage for your needs.

- If choosing a harness, look for one that attaches itself to the seat belt. It should go round the dog's chest, back and shoulders. A cage can also be used for big dogs. Make sure it's properly secured with a seat belt. A dog guard is not recommended – although it will keep the pet away from the driver, it will not protect the animal in a crash.

- Small dogs, cats and other pets can be transported in a pet carrier. Hold this in place with a seat belt or wedge it in on the floor of the car. Don't put a carrier in the boot of a saloon car – the animal could suffocate.

- Even the most docile of pets can get agitated during a car journey. Some owners recommend putting a self-scented material at the bottom of the carrier to calm pets down.

- Finally, never leave your pets in a stationary vehicle on a hot day. They will quickly dehydrate and could die.

Road Sense: Get Car Savvy

Good driving is more than skill. And it's more than having a rudimentary knowledge of basic maintenance and repairs (which you can now pass with flying colours, of course). Good driving is all about common sense, protecting yourself and considering others on the road. Always remember that a car has the potential to be a lethal weapon. Those who have just passed their test should be particularly careful – the combination of false confidence and inexperience means that new drivers have the highest proportion of deaths. But driving doesn't have to be a chore. Here are some pointers to having a fun time on the road . . .

Other safety issues

- Always make sure that you and your passengers are wearing a seat belt – it's the law. Wear the belt correctly and ensure it's not twisted. If you're pregnant, the lap strap should rest under your bump, not across it.

- Consider your vehicle's climate control. Make sure your heater and air conditioning are always working correctly. It's important you feel comfortable while driving – chilly toes could hamper your concentration. If your car has a heated seat, switch it on for frosty mornings. And if it's damp, set the demister on high for the windscreen and side windows.

- Always do regular maintenance checks (see pages 44–45).

- Plan your route before setting off to avoid any unnecessary distractions when driving.

- Be prepared: always carry a basic tool kit, warning triangle, fire extinguisher and so forth (see pages 20–21 for full list).

Defensive driving

Defensive driving means being aware of what's going on around you at all times, using your mirrors constantly and learning to read the road ahead. What's that cyclist doing? Is that car about to turn? There are several other factors you should consider, such as the weather, the traffic flow and the quality of light. When driving, you must also be in a stable frame of mind: don't drive when angry, off-colour, distracted or drunk. You want to be in control at all times.

Certain journeys can affect your quality of driving. Commuting the same route every day, for instance, can produce feelings of lethargy. Prevent this by changing your route occasionally, or even changing the time you travel. The saying holds true: a change is as good as a rest.

Long-distance driving is another safety issue. Make sure you stop regularly, stretch your legs and get some air. Don't forget to eat and drink plenty of fluid. And try avoiding sugary foods – after the initial rush, you will swiftly feel sluggish.

Road rage

To avoid the wrath of other drivers, remember to stick to the laws of the road: signal clearly, keep to the speed limits and keep your distance behind another vehicle.

If you feel you have done something wrong, acknowledge your mistake to the other road user. If, however, you end up being pursued by an angry driver, avoid making any eye contact (this could provoke further anger) and, if possible, jot down the registration, make and model of car. Make sure your doors and windows are all locked. If you feel that you could be in danger, phone the police. If possible, stop in a built-up, busy area to do this.

Are you the one feeling the rage? Take a deep breath and put the situation into context – don't take someone else's bad driving personally. Never retaliate – it really isn't worth it.

All-Weather Driving: Whatever the Weather

Again, you drivers win the luck of the road draw as, unlike bikers or cyclists, you're not as exposed to the elements. Of course, your car is, so remember to adapt your technique, ensure your car is in tip-top condition and factor in any journey delays. Check the forecast before setting out to find out if it's likely to get worse. And if the weather is truly terrible, try not to drive at all.

Snow

Many countries are badly affected by the first winter snowfall. Why? Because they're simply not used to it. Similarly, any drivers who aren't used to snow should be particularly cautious. The first fall of snow is especially dangerous as this is before the roads have been gritted. Once they have, they can still be very slippery – and remember, maintenance fans, that salty grit can cause rust.

Always clear any snow from your windows and windscreen before setting out, check your lights and mirrors are clear and your number plates are visible. Drive more slowly than normal, allowing for longer stopping distances. Test your brakes gently soon after starting off.

If you break down in freezing conditions, adhere to the number one breakdown rule: STAY WITH YOUR CAR. Your vehicle will always be easier to find than you. Keep the heater on and wait for help.

Ice

Ice is worse still, especially since it's often hard to spot. The worst offender is black ice, almost invisible ice patches on a normally good road surface. Thankfully, you can suss out if black ice is about: if the road looks wet, but your tyres aren't acting the way they would normally with rain, it's probably black ice. Drive extremely slowly. If possible, don't drive at all.

Tips for a winter wonderland

AS TEMPTING AS IT IS TO TOAST YOURSELF IN FRONT OF AN OPEN FIRE DURING THE WINTER MONTHS, YOU REALLY CAN'T BE A HERMIT. SO PREPARE YOURSELF FOR WINTER DRIVING, FOR THE SNOW, ICE AND FREEZING TEMPERATURES. YOU NEVER KNOW WHEN A SHOVEL MIGHT COME IN HANDY.

- When driving in winter, always leave with a full tank of fuel. Fuel-consumption soars in cold weather.

- Always carry a winter survival kit: a couple of blankets, a can of de-icer, a scraper, a tow rope and a shovel.

- Never be tempted to clear your frosty windscreen with a kettle of boiling water – it's dangerous and potentially damaging. Use the de-icer and scraper.

- Do thorough and frequent checks of the following: the coolant (if it freezes, your engine will be in trouble), the battery (which will be strained from the extra use of lights, wipers and demister), the wipers and the washer reservoir levels.

- Snow chains are needed only in severe conditions. However, they are necessary on many mountain roads. Make sure you know how to use them before setting off. It may also be compulsory to remove them when you return to driving on good ground.

If you skid, don't slam your foot down on the brake. Instead, decrease your acceleration and, using the steering wheel, turn your car in the desired direction. Once it's stopped skidding and your car has turned, move your wheel to the central position. Correct any skidding in the opposite direction in the same manner. This way you're pulling your car out of a skid.

Fog

Fog is another baddie – not only is your visibility affected, but other road users will also have difficulty seeing your vehicle. Fog has a tendency to go from a hazy mist to an impenetrable blanket in an instant. If visibility is really bad, use front foglights or dipped headlights as well as your rear foglights. Keep your windscreen wipers and demister on. Drive slowly, but, if possible, don't drive at all.

Rain

Again, this calls for you to be alert and to lower your speed – brakes and tyres are much less effective when wet, and stopping distances will be at least double. Slow down gradually to avoid skidding. Use your wipers and demister, and don't be shy about switching on your headlights – rain will reduce visibility.

Rain is particularly dangerous following a prolonged dry spell – the water loosens all the oil and other gunk on the road, causing oil slicks to form. Another danger is aquaplaning. This is where a layer of water forms between your tyres and the road surface and you lose control. The solution? Don't drive too fast.

 Greasy Gloria

Steamy windows will get other drivers talking – and for all the wrong reasons – so always carry a clean cloth and use the heater 'demist' setting. And it goes without saying that you'll have a breakdown kit in the boot of your car (see pages 20–21) – you'll really need it when the weather turns nasty.

Roadside Situations: If It All Goes Wrong . . .

You can maintain, prepare and repair all you like, but you can't predict an accident or, indeed, a breakdown. Both do happen, even to the most virtuous of drivers. Here's what to do ...

If your car breaks down:

1 Pull over and stop immediately. Make sure you park away from any oncoming traffic. Switch on the hazard lights and set up the warning triangle.

2 Isolate and diagnose the problem. Be honest, now – can you solve it? If not, call a vehicle rescue organisation (hopefully with the mobile phone you should always carry with you).

3 Stay inside the car – unless there's a danger of other vehicles hitting it – with the doors and windows locked. Wait for assistance.

4 If you break down on a motorway, pull onto the hard shoulder and switch on the hazard lights. Leave the vehicle using the passenger door. Telephone for assistance. In this instance, don't get back inside the car unless you personally feel at risk. Fatal crashes on the hard shoulder are not uncommon.

Greasy Gloria

It's really worth joining a breakdown assistance organisation. Not only does it offer peace of mind – particularly for women – but it will also pay for itself after the first call-out. A mobile phone is another must. Always remember to carry a pen and paper with you in your glove box – if you're involved in an accident, you'll need to jot down any names/details.

If someone is injured, remember:

A Airways must be cleared of any obstruction.

B Breathing must be maintained. If there is no breathing, attempt mouth-to-mouth resuscitation.

C Blood circulation must be maintained and any bleeding stopped with a firm pressure using clean material if possible.

If you find yourself at the scene of an accident:

1 Further collisions may happen, so warn other traffic by switching on your hazard lights or by placing a warning triangle in the road.

2 Call the emergency services if necessary.

3 Manage any injured parties in the following way:

- Move injured people away from the vehicle/s and into a safe place, BUT don't move people unnecessarily. Don't move people who are trapped inside a vehicle unless they're in danger (such as from fire).

- If you're dealing with a biker, don't remove the helmet.

- If carrying a first aid kit, use a bandage to stem any heavy bleeding.

4 If you see an accident and there are already enough people involved, continue driving – you may be more of a hindrance than a help.

If you are involved in a road accident

EVEN IF IT'S NOT YOUR FAULT, IF YOU ARE INVOLVED IN AN ACCIDENT THERE ARE CERTAIN STEPS YOU MUST TAKE – OTHERWISE, YOU COULD BE BREAKING THE LAW.

1. The law requires you to stop. As before, warn other traffic to prevent further collisions by switching on hazard lights or placing a warning triangle in the road.

2. Switch off the engine.

3. If someone is injured, call the emergency services.

4. Call the police if: someone is hurt; you've damaged someone's property, but you can't find them to tell them; the road is blocked with debris; or if someone leaves the scene of the accident without exchanging details.

5. Get the names, addresses and phone numbers (avoid mobiles) of any witnesses.

6. Get the name, address and phone number of the other party. Also get insurance details and ask if he/she is the owner of the vehicle.

7. Note down the make, model, colour and registration number of the other vehicle/s involved. Also make a note of the damage sustained.

8. And jot down any other pertinent details: weather conditions, road conditions, what everyone involved said, whether the other party's lights/indicators were on, and so forth.

9. Make a note of the exact location of the collision and how it happened. It can help to draw a map while the situation is still clear in your mind, or if you have a camera, take photos.

10. Be nice to the other party, even if they're acting like a monster. But do not discuss liability – and under no circumstances admit it.

11. If the police ask for a statement, you do not have to make one straightaway. It is often better to make one later on when any shock has subsided. And think about your wording very carefully – consult a solicitor or your motoring organisation if you are really worried.

Learn the Lingo

However confident you now feel as an amateur mechanic, you can't do everything yourself. Many women find visiting a garage or body shop somewhat daunting – all that jargon and male bravado flying around among the spare parts. Read on for some tips on how to handle the professionals, and a little more about all the new terminology you'll need to know. That way you can nod knowledgeably if someone starts referring to your crankshaft.

Dealing with the professionals

Try and use a mechanic recommended by a friend. If this isn't possible, shop around for the best quote – remember that you shouldn't be charged for the initial examination – and ask for a written quotation before work gets started. It's best to use a garage that specialises in your particular make of car. If your car is still under warranty, remember always to take it to an authorised dealer. You can still use an authorised dealer after the warranty has expired, but this tends to be more costly than a local garage.

Also do your homework. Find out the price of any parts that need replacing – call your car manufacturer if necessary to ask the recommended retail price. This way you'll know if you're paying a fair price for the repairs. It's also worth asking the mechanic to return the old parts to you when your car has been repaired – you can be sure then that you're actually getting new parts.

On payment, go through the bill carefully. Make sure it is itemised and question any additional costs immediately. Don't leave upset and return the following day – they could argue that when you left you were perfectly happy. Clear up any problems immediately.

Alternator
The generator that supplies electricity to the car's electrical system. The power is driven when the engine is running.

ABS
Abbreviation for anti-lock braking system, which most newer cars have. This stops the wheels from locking – and thus going into a skid – when you brake heavily.

Allen key
A six-sided L-shaped slot-in tool that comes in a set of varying sizes; good for adjustments to recessed bolts.

Bearing
A tough surface – usually metal – against which another part moves. The aim is to minimise friction between fixed and moving parts.

Booster seat
A type of child's seat that 'boosts' the height of the child, enabling him or her to wear the seat belt correctly.

Brake pads
Rubber-based pads that touch the brake disks or drums when the brake lever is applied.

Carburettor
Part of the fuel system, this mixes the fuel with the air so it will ignite.

Choke
This can decrease the volume of air that enters the carburettor when the engine starts from cold.

Coolant
A mixture of water and anti-freeze.

Crankshaft
The part of the engine that translates the motion of the pistons and connecting rods into a rotary action. This then starts the car wheels moving.

Cylinder
The part of the engine where the fuel/air mixture is burned to provide power to drive the machine.

Dipstick
Device for checking the oil level.

Drivebelt
Another name for the fan belt.

Drivetrain
Describes the engine, clutch, gearbox and driveshaft – in other words, everything that is used to transmit drive to the wheels.

WD40
Prevents corrosion and gets rid of dampness in engines.

Estate
Type of car, longer than a hatchback or saloon.

Fan belt
Transmits drive between two sprockets. Resembles a belt and is usually rubber.

Fuel-injection system
You car will either have this or a carburettor. Both perform the same function, mixing fuel with air.

Hatchback
Car body type. Hatchbacks have foldable rear seats and a sloping rear 'hatch' instead of a boot.

Hubcap
Covers the bolts on your wheels.

Jack
Lifts up the car so you can change the wheel.

Km/l
Short for kilometres per litre. One method of measuring a car's fuel economy.

MPG
Short for miles per gallon. Another way to measure a car's fuel economy.

MPV
Abbreviation for multi-purpose vehicle. Has a high driving position and can carry up to seven passengers.

Odometer
Counts the number of kilometres/miles your car has been driven.

Piston
A cylindrical contraption that slides neatly into a cylinder. Found in the engine.

Rev
Short for revolutions. The engine speed is measured in revs per minute – RPM.

Saloon
Distinctive car body type with a separate boot.

Spark plug
This provides the spark that ignites the air/fuel mixture in the engine.

Tachometer
Registers the engine speed in revs (revolutions) per minute (RPM).

Top box
A form of storage attached to two rails on the car roof.

Torque wrench
A specially designed wrench that makes a loud click when the exact amount of force required for the nut and bolt has been applied, preventing you from over- or under-tightening the joint.

Tracking system
A security device in which a satellite system helps pinpoint a stolen vehicle.

Transmission
Used to describe all the drivetrain components with the exception of the engine.

Tread gauge
Measures the tyre tread.

Tyre pressure gauge
Vital for checking your tyre pressure.

Washer reservoir
Stores the washer fluid used by the wipers to clean your windscreen.

Wheel brace
Essential for removing wheel nuts. Ones with extending handles are easier to use.

Women Drivers!

OK, so this is not a driving technique book. But since it's aimed at women – and, we hope, in a non-patronising, non-sexist way – we thought we should briefly refer to a couple of common driving problems suffered by women (and, of course, men). We all know that women are involved in fewer crashes and have fewer speeding tickets, but that doesn't mean everything is an easy ride. Here are how to do two of the most difficult manoeuvres in style.

Reverse parking

In a busy street, between two vehicles, this is really parking under pressure, especially when you have an audience watching and a backlog of traffic behind you. Take it steady and try and get into the space in one go. Don't feel rushed – otherwise you will have to reposition yourself again.

1 First indicate and brake just before the gap. Don't move ahead of the gap or the car behind you might move into the space. Make sure you have adequate space – you need one and a half times the length of your own vehicle.

It's tow joke . . .

ONE DAY – THE SHAME! – YOUR CAR MIGHT NEED TO BE TOWED AWAY. ALWAYS CARRY A TOW ROPE IN YOUR BOOT FOR THIS VERY REASON.

- The front and rear of the car should have something called a 'toeing eye'. Check your car handbook for details on how to find it.

- The ignition key should be turned to 'on'. This releases the steering lock and allows the lights to work. If the battery is flat, use hand signals. If you drive an automatic, move the gear lever to 'N'.

- The tow rope should be kept tight at all times between the broken-down vehicle and the towing car. This might require the driver of the broken-down vehicle to brake frequently, but carefully. You will have to press harder on the brake pedal than usual.

- Drive slowly, and discuss the route before setting off.

---

2 Now move and stop ahead of the gap, about one metre (3ft) ahead of it. Select reverse gear.

3 Start reversing. When your rear is level with the end of the front car, turn the wheel one and a half times.

4 Then, when your door mirror lines up with the end of the other car, turn the wheel one and a half times the other way.

5 Continue reversing. When you see the offside corner of the other car, turn your wheel one and a half times to the right.

6 Now you should be almost parallel with the kerb. Turn the wheel one and a half times to the left to straighten up.

7 Stop!

Turning in the road

Taxi drivers have this down to a fine art; for everyone else, this can be a nightmare.

1 Steer the car across the road, preferably aiming for a 90-degree angle to the kerb. Try to get your wheel into a full right lock in the shortest distance possible.

2 About a metre (3ft) from the kerb, steer quickly the other way. Brake before you hit the kerb. Put on the handbrake.

3 Then reverse, steering quickly to the left. Again, about a metre (3ft) from the kerb, start steering to the right. Brake and put the handbrake on.

4 Now, if you're lucky, you have turned in the road and can move forward. If not, repeat the manoeuvre again – very few 'three-point turns' are done in three turns!

Driving Abroad: All Aboard!

It might sound daft, but the point of a holiday is to relax. If you're driving, then, you should aim to make it as hassle-free as possible. The key here is preparation, for instance familiarising yourself with the driving laws of the country you're about to visit. Some other pointers to consider are . . .

- Have a full service before setting out. If you get any new parts fitted, wait for them to settle down – this could take a few weeks.

- Always carry your driving licence. Many non-EU countries require an International Driving Permit (although you must take your other licence as well). Italy requires either a translation with your licence or an International Driving Permit.

- You'll need other documentation too. Always carry your vehicle registration document, vehicle test certificate and insurance documents. You may need to take out additional insurance cover – tell your company where you're going and ask their advice.

- Carry a few more tools than normal – in fact, as many as you can hold. Stow away the usual spares like fuses, and a fan belt. Always, always take your car handbook.

- In some countries it is a legal requirement to carry a spare set of bulbs, a warning triangle and a first aid kit. All are worth carrying anyway.

- Find out about the rules and regulations of the country you'll be travelling in before setting off. A good website to check out is www.drivingabroad.co.uk.

- There are also different regulations for children and child seats. For more details, visit the Royal Society for the Prevention of Accidents website at www.childseats.org.uk/countries.

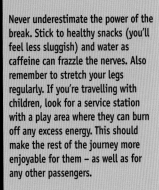

Greasy Gloria

Never underestimate the power of the break. Stick to healthy snacks (you'll feel less sluggish) and water as caffeine can frazzle the nerves. Also remember to stretch your legs regularly. If you're travelling with children, look for a service station with a play area where they can burn off any excess energy. This should make the rest of the journey more enjoyable for them – as well as for any other passengers.

- There can also be different laws for towing caravans and trailers abroad. In some countries you must adhere to strict speed limits. You may also need a separate warning light attached to the car to show the trailer indicator lights are working.

- Remember to display your nationality on the back of your car.

- When driving on the opposite side of the road for the first time, be especially careful. Remember that your headlights will no longer dip correctly. Attach deflector triangles to redirect most of the glare.

- Make sure your luggage is secure and don't overload your vehicle. If carrying a heavy load, use the appropriate equipment (see pages 46–47 for more details). When parking, don't leave any luggage on show.

- Prepare, prepare, prepare. Plan the journey and don't take on more than you're capable of. Have plenty of breaks, especially if you're driving at dusk when accidents are most likely to occur, or in the early hours of the morning.

- It's highly recommended that you join a breakdown organisation. Not only can they help you out in the case of a major breakdown when your car may need to be shipped home, but they can also tell you about necessary documentation, traffic regulations and road tolls, and advise you on your route.

- Bon voyage!

2 Wheels

Tyres and wheels:
Wheel types include spoked, alloy and pressed steel.

Drive chain:
Channels the power from the engine to the rear wheel.

Battery:
Provides power to start the engine, and for the lights, indicators and horn.

Engine:
The engine will be either two-stroke or four-stroke.

'You are as brave as a motorcycle.'
US POET ANNE SEXTON

Throttle:
Increases or decreases the engine's revs.

Braking system:
Either mechanically or hydraulically operated.

Steering head bearings:
For smooth steering and good control.

Clutch:
Lever on the left that enables you to change gear.

What Motorcycle Should I Buy?

Gwyneth Paltrow's no fool: the savvy scooter girl has sussed that the best way to get round town is on two wheels. Nearly one in ten of all motorcyclists, be it leathered-up bikers or ped-heads like Gwynnie, are now women. But what should you go for? And how much power do you need? Here's the low-down on which bike is right for you and your lifestyle.

BUY-A-BIKE

Learner

✓ Good for

The novice. As the name suggests, these bikes are perfect for the beginner. They are surprisingly powerful, too.

✖ Bad for

Intermediate riders. This bike has its sell-by date – sooner or later you'll want to move on to bigger things.

Commuter

✓ Good for

The cost conscious. They're cheap to run so perfect if you're on an economy drive. Also good for short journeys.

✖ Bad for

Speed demons. These are low-powered machines. Commuter bikes don't really do great distances either – they're aimed at commuters rather than travellers.

Scooter

✓ Good for

Nipping around cities. If you're looking for a reliable motorised alternative to public transport, this is it.

✖ Bad for

Cruising across country. This is the smallest (many scooters only have a 50cc engine) and least powerful (the maximum speed of a 50cc scooter is 31mph) of the bunch.

Trail

✓ Good for

The observant. The high seat and handlebars give you an upright riding position, making it easy to see the road ahead.

✖ Bad for

(Initially) urbanites. As these were designed for off-road use, urban riders should fit road tyres. Then, with its excellent suspension and riding position, urban riders will have the perfect city bike.

BUY-A-BIKE

Sports

✓ Good for

Girl racers who like to be seen. The sports bike is all about good looks and super-fast speeds.

✖ Bad for

Penny pinchers. You'll need money to burn for this one: the sports bike is expensive to buy and run.

Touring

✓ Good for

Those who travel *a deux*. Plus the fat, squishy seat and luggage space makes this the perfect machine for long distances.

✖ Bad for

Saturday shoppers. Come on now: how silly would you look riding this to the local mall.

Cruiser

✓ Good for

Easy riders. This is a distinctive-looking bike with a low body and high handlebars (think Harley-Davidson). Comes in a variety of engine sizes.

✖ Bad for

Chicks on speed. As the style suggests, this is a laid-back bike in every sense.

Retro

✓ Good for

The super-cool. Retro bikes are modern machines based on old-school designs. Great if you don't like plastic.

✖ Bad for

Technophiles. Although these bikes are reliable – as opposed to a genuine vintage machine – they're not necessarily hi-tech.

Know Your Motorcycle

What's a Throttle?

You've plumped for the scooter, then. Or maybe you're more of a laid-back cruiser kind of girl. If you struggle to recognise your engine from your battery, however, you won't be going far.

Although a scooter may look very different from a cruiser, both operate using similar parts and similar principles. But there are some variations on the biking theme. The

1 **THROTTLE:** This is the device that makes the engine increase or decrease its revs, which in turn makes the bike go faster or slower. Comes with either a single or twin cable.

2 **CLUTCH:** The clutch enables the rider to change gear – but not on an automatic, where instead the left-hand lever controls the rear brake. The clutch will be either cable- or hydraulically operated.

3 **SUSPENSION AND STEERING:** Made up of the handlebars, front forks, shock absorbers and steering head bearings, all of which contribute towards a comfortable ride. The bearings must be correctly adjusted or steering control will be affected.

4 **BATTERY:** This provides the power to start the engine, and run the lights, indicators and horn. Many lucky owners have bikes with maintenance-free batteries, so no tinkering is required.

5 **WHEELS AND TYRES:** Wheels come in three types: spoked, alloy and pressed steel. It is crucial they run 'true', otherwise the tyres will wear rapidly and the bike will be unstable. Tyres must be correctly inflated and have a minimum tread of 1mm (¹⁄₂₅in).

6 **BRAKING SYSTEM:** There are two types of system: mechanically operated and hydraulically operated. Brake pads and shoes must be checked and replaced regularly.

7 **ENGINE:** Two-stroke engines use petrol and oil, while four-stroke engines generally run on unleaded fuel and are smoother at lower speeds. Within these categories, engines are then classified according to the number of cylinders and their engine capacity.

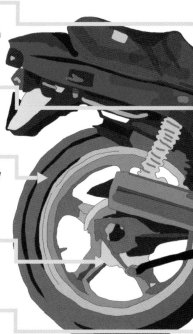

Before you get on the road, get a licence that permits you to ride. In the UK that means you must be at least 17 years old (16 for a moped).

- You have the choice of a provisional driving licence, full driving car licence or a provisional motorcycle licence. This will allow you to ride with L-plates, although you can't take a passenger or go on a motorway.

- You will also need to complete your Compulsory Basic Training (CBT) at an approved organisation. CBT will teach you about theory and road safety skills. After passing, you can ride solo on a bike of up to 125cc.

- You can then take a practical test and go for one of the full licences: full moped, full category A motorcycle or full sub-category A1 light motorcycle.

engine, for instance, can be simple and two-stroke (running on a mixture of petrol and oil) or more complex and four-stroke (these generally run on unleaded fuel). Likewise, some bikes have gears while others incorporate automatic transmission. Below is a rough guide to what bits go where – and what they do.

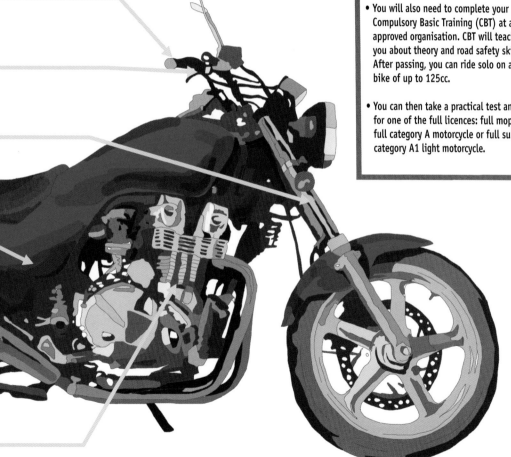

Know Your Motorcycle

Be in Control

A thorough knowledge of your motorcycle's controls is vital before setting off: where they are, what they do, and how they work. Controls vary from bike to bike, but the following should give you a general idea – and stop you from landing in a ditch.

Left handlebar controls

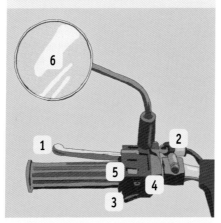

1 **CLUTCH LEVER:** Controls the clutch. This is not found on automatic machines, where instead this is the rear brake lever.

2 **CHOKE:** Helps get the bike going when you start up the engine from cold.

3 **HORN:** So you can be heard as well as seen.

4 **INDICATORS:** Used when changing direction.

5 **HEADLIGHT FLASHER:** To flash your headlights.

6 **MIRRORS:** Make sure they're properly adjusted.

Right handlebar controls

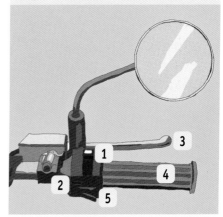

1 **ELECTRIC STARTER:** Used as well as, or instead of, the kick-starter (see foot controls).

2 **ENGINE CUT-OUT SWITCH:** To stop the engine in an emergency; under normal circumstances, use the ignition switch.

3 **FRONT BRAKE LEVER:** Squeeze the lever to slow or stop the front wheel.

4 **THROTTLE:** Twisting this towards you increases the engine's speed; away from you it slows it down.

5 **LIGHT SWITCH:** Operates headlights and parking lights.

Left and right foot controls

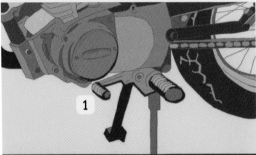

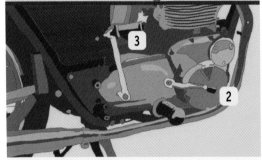

Note that these controls are for a motorcycle with gears and that automatics don't have foot controls.

1 GEAR SELECTOR: Positioned just in front of the foot rest, this allows the rider to change gears.

2 REAR BRAKE PEDAL: Again in front of the footrest, but this time on the right side, the rear brake pedal applies the brake to the rear wheel.

3 KICK-STARTER: Stamp down on this repeatedly until the engine starts.

Instrument panel

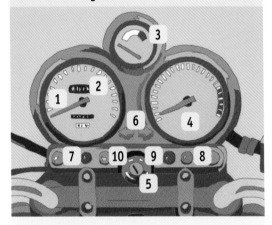

1 SPEEDOMETER: Tells you your speed.

2 MILEOMETER: Shows how many miles you have travelled.

3 TEMPERATURE GAUGE: Shows temperature of coolant.

4 REV COUNTER: Displays engine revolutions per minute.

5 IGNITION SWITCH: Turn the key to get your bike going.

6 INDICATOR REPEATERS: Flash when indicators are on.

7 OIL PRESSURE LAMP: Warns of low engine oil pressure.

8 HIGH BEAM LAMP: Lights when headlamp is on full beam.

9 IGNITION LAMP: Lights up when you switch on ignition.

10 NEUTRAL LAMP: Indicates gear is in neutral position.

Basic Motorcycle Kit

You don't have to worry about what to wear too much in a car. A motorcycle, on the other hand, requires a total wardrobe rethink. Flip-flops and hippy skirts are absolute no-nos; your new style icon should be the leathered-up Marianne Faithfull in *Girl on a Motorcycle* (sorry vegetarians, but leather really is better than the man-made alternatives). Scooters are more forgiving, although a protective jacket, boots and long trousers are recommended in case you ever suffer a fall.

WATERPROOF JACKET	LEATHERS	BOOTS	GLOVES/GAUNTLETS	GOGGLES/ FACE SHIELD	SOCKS

Man-made outfits should be bright and warm. Most are made to fit over your clothes.	Expensive, but offer protection and are windproof. Have padding at elbows and shoulders.	Trainers just won't do as they will offer no protection if you fall. Leather boots are best.	Always ride with a pair of these to protect you from the elements plus improve your grip.	Protects your eyes from the weather, flying insects and dirt. Replace immediately when scratched.	Because riding can get very chilly. Invest in a super-thick pair.

Helmet help

This is the one thing you absolutely can't be without and is a legal requirement for motorcycling in the UK. A reputable dealer will stock a wide range of helmets that will comply with all the necessary safety standards.

• Helmets come in two styles: full-face or open-face. Full-face is best as it offers better protection. Open-face helmets must be worn with either a visor or goggles – this type won't protect your chin but is worth trying if you're claustrophobic.

• Helmets are made from three different types of material: polycarbonate, which is light and cheap but won't last long; fibreglass, which will last longer but weighs more; and Kevlar, both tough and light, hence the most expensive option.

• When buying a helmet, check the fit: if it's loose, it's unsafe. A helmet can be fastened in three ways: double d-ring, quick release or bar and buckle.

• If your helmet becomes damaged – however minor the knock – buy a new one as it may no longer be structurally sound.

REFLECTIVE TAPE

Stick it all over you and your bike as you want to be as visible as possible.

LOCK

Invest in something heavy-duty like a U-lock or a chain lock (pictured).

WINDSCREENS/WINDSHIELD

Protects your face and body from the weather.

HANDLEBAR MUFFS

Keep your hands warm and dry so you'll feel more comfortable when you ride.

FAIRING

Made from heavy-duty materials such as fibreglass, fairings protect the rider from the elements.

ANTI-FOG SOLUTION

Vital to prevent goggles from misting up in wet or cold weather.

CLEAN CLOTH

Because you never know when you'll need to pull over and clean your goggles.

LUGGAGE STRAPS

Used with a luggage rack. For more protection, consider a pannier or box.

Tool Box Essentials

So you've bought the bike, the clothes, and the accessories. Your next purchase? Some tools. Most bikes are sold with a basic tool kit – this won't be enough. Since basic motorcycle maintenance really isn't that tricky (we promise), it's worth forking out for the tools on the facing page. But first, a few tips . . .

 Greasy Gloria

Don't leave home without . . .

Since you're not psychic (we're guessing) and you can't predict a breakdown, carry the following with you at all times. If you don't have space for everything, ensure you at least have your mobile phone with you to call for assistance.

Mobile phone, in case of emergencies

Spare bulbs

Spare fuses

A spare inner tube (if your tyres are tubed)

Torch

Water bottle

Swiss Army knife

A compact tool kit containing: a socket set, spanners, screwdrivers, insulating tape, nuts, bolts, washers and a set of Allen keys

A clean cloth for wiping your visor or goggles

Your machine's handbook

Quality counts

When purchasing your tool kit, spend as much money on the tools as your budget will allow. Quality tools will definitely last longer – they may well last a whole lifetime – whereas cheap tools are liable to break and could actually damage your machine. And you really don't want that.

Learn workshop skills

Always use the right tool for the job – and use it correctly. A process of trial and error (with hopefully few errors) should help you with this. When using a spanner, for example, always turn the tool towards you to minimise the likelihood of injury. Oh, and ring spanners or sockets are generally better than open-ended ones as they offer more grip. But again, you'll pick up tips like this with a bit of practice.

But don't ever use too much force – and this applies to both tightening and untightening nuts and bolts. If you are using a hammer, make sure that it is covered with a cloth, and be gentle. Better still, use a soft-faced mallet – this is far less likely to damage any of the components on your bike.

Dress for dirt

Wear an outfit that you don't mind being splattered in oil – overalls, available from most DIY stores, are perfect attire. Tie your hair back, remove any jewellery and wear a pair of plastic gloves – some of the liquids you will be dealing with are particularly corrosive. And always have a pile of clean cloths and newspapers on hand to mop up any spillages.

While working, you should also protect your machine from dirt, in particular the engine. Let the tinkering begin!

Tools of the trade

BELOW IS WHAT YOU'LL NEED TO MAKE YOUR DREAM OF MOTORCYCLE MAINTENANCE A REALITY. STORE THE TOOLS TOGETHER IN YOUR GARAGE, IDEALLY IN A STRONG TOOL BOX.

INSULATING TAPE: For bandaging-up jobs in an emergency before taking your machine to a mechanic.

SPANNERS: Don't skimp, and invest in an entire set to cover all eventualities.

TORCH: You'll need this to see clearly in any hard-to-reach places.

TORQUE WRENCH: For tightening nuts and bolts. Wait for the loud click – this indicates the predetermined setting.

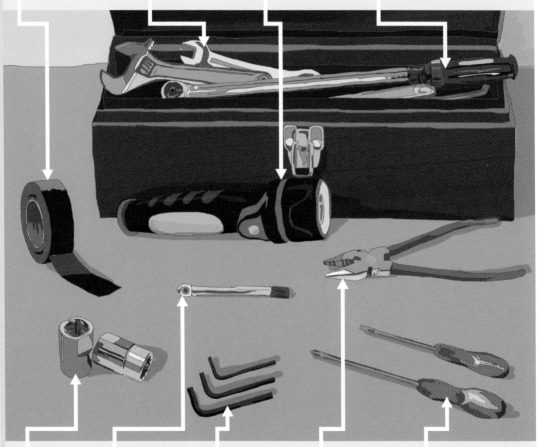

SOCKETS: Essential for loosening tight bolts.

TYRE-PRESSURE GAUGE: Vital to check your tyres are the right pressure.

SET OF ALLEN KEYS: To fit and adjust bolts.

PLIERS: Much stronger than simply using your hands.

SCREWDRIVERS: You'll need a selection of both Phillips and flat-blade screwdrivers.

Motorcycle Science: Understanding Your Machine

To do even the most basic maintenance and repairs on your bike, you'll need a crash course in elementary mechanics. And that starts with understanding how the engine works. Here goes: in very plain English.

The basic function of an engine is to burn fuel to produce the power that drives the machine. There are two types of engine; their differences relate to the design and the way they produce power. Two-stroke engines run on a mixture of petrol and oil, the ratios of which vary from bike to bike. They have a simpler design than a

Petrol and electrics

How does the fuel system work?

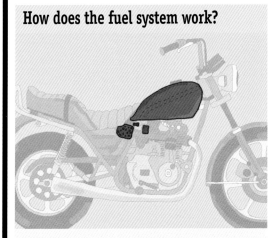

The fuel system includes a tank (to store petrol), a carburettor (to mix the petrol with air so it will ignite) and a petrol tap (to control the petrol flow from tank to carburettor). The petrol/air mixture is carried to the engine's cylinders where it is burned to provide power to drive the machine.

The throttle (situated on the right handlebar) controls the amount of fuel directed to the engine. This essentially controls the engine's (and therefore the bike's) speed and power. To speed up the engine, turn the throttle towards you. To slow it down, twist it the other way.

What happens when I turn the key?

First you must ensure that the fuel tap, the choke (which changes the amount of air in the petrol/air mixture that the engine burns) and the cut-out switch are all on. Turning the ignition key completes an electrical circuit that results in the petrol/air mixture in the engine's cylinder being ignited.

However, damp can cause problems with the ignition system. To prevent this, protect the ignition system with a water-repellent spray, though don't apply spray to the actual switch. You should also ensure that your spark plugs are properly adjusted and in full working order. Next, depending on your bike, you either press the electric starter button or tread sharply on the kick-starter. You're now ready to move off.

four-stroke engine but a higher fuel consumption. Four-stroke engines, on the other hand, generally run on unleaded fuel and are smoother at low speeds. Within these categories, engines are then classified according to the number of cylinders and their engine capacity. Multi-cylinder bikes are usually larger and more powerful, hence good for long-distance riding. And the bigger the engine capacity, the more powerful the machine – indeed, some bikes have the same engine capacity as a small car.

Gears and gases

And how do I move?

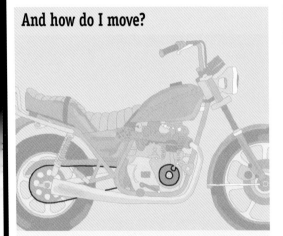

Movement is thanks to the transmission system – this transmits the drive from the engine to the rear wheel. The transmission system consists of a drive chain (similar to a bicycle chain), and a clutch and gearbox that control the machine's speed.

What about the oil?
The oil plays no part in the engine combustion process. Instead it serves to lubricate the moving parts of the engine reducing friction, keeping the engine cool and preventing rust and corrosion. Make sure you use the correct grade and keep it at the right level.

What does the exhaust pipe do?

The exhaust system consists of a pipe linked up to the exhaust port of the engine, and a silencer, which reduces noise levels (incidentally, this is a legal requirement). The exhaust removes waste gases from the engine – if it makes it any easier to understand, compare it to the human body!

Basic Maintenance and Repairs

Even though motorcycles make up just two per cent of the traffic flow, they're involved in more than 20 per cent of all accidents. Scary stuff. But since many accidents are caused by bad bike maintenance, a once-over on a regular basis should reduce the chance of you becoming a statistic. Luckily, the art of motorcycle maintenance requires no zen, just a little common sense – and some overalls would be good as it can get messy. Here's what you should be doing . . .

Chore Chart: What to do when

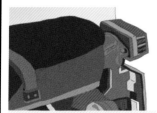

DAILY:

- TEST ALL THE LIGHTS: FRONT, REAR, SIDE, BOTH INDICATORS AND BRAKE
- CHECK THE CHAIN IS SECURE
- MAKE SURE THE TYRES CONTAIN NO STRAY DEBRIS (EG, NAILS, STONES)
- TEST THAT THE BRAKES WORK BY SQUEEZING THE FRONT BRAKE LEVER
- CHECK THE FUEL AND OIL

WEEKLY:

- EXAMINE THE DRIVE CHAIN: IT SHOULD BE NEITHER TOO SLACK NOR TOO TIGHT
- CHECK THE STEERING HEAD BEARINGS FOR SMOOTH STEERING MOVEMENT. IF THE ADJUSTMENT IS WONKY, YOUR BIKE WILL BE DIFFICULT TO CONTROL
- TEST YOUR TYRES' PRESSURE AND TREAD
- CHECK YOUR HORN'S HOOTING, ALTHOUGH NOT AT 2AM IN A RESIDENTIAL AREA
- MAKE SURE EVERY VISIBLE NUT AND BOLT IS TIGHT

FORTNIGHTLY:

- TEST OUT THE SUSPENSION BY SITTING ON THE BIKE AND BOUNCING UP AND DOWN
- GIVE THE BATTERY A ONCE-OVER
- CHECK FOR ANY OIL LEAKING FROM THE SHOCK ABSORBERS AND FRONT FORKS
- INSPECT THE THROTTLE – THAT IT CLOSES PROPERLY WHEN RELEASED AND THAT THE CABLES AREN'T FRAYED
- IF THE CLUTCH IS HYDRAULICALLY OPERATED, CHECK THE FLUID LEVEL AND LOOK OUT FOR LEAKS
- CHECK BRAKE FLUID LEVEL AND PADS
- FOR LIQUID-COOLED ENGINES, MAKE SURE THE COOLANT LEVEL IS BETWEEN THE MINIMUM AND MAXIMUM MARKS
- IF THE BIKE HAS A CENTRE STAND YOU CAN CHECK THE WHEELS ARE RUNNING CORRECTLY BY SPINNING EACH ONE
- CLEAN YOUR BIKE

Greasy Gloria's No-Nos

1. Never skip on checking the oil

How else do you expect your bike to run? Check the oil when the engine is cold and the bike completely upright; park it on its stand. You'll also need a spare rag to hand as this is a messy business. Your bike will either have a dipstick or a sightglass as a means of monitoring the oil level. Do this every day before setting off. Forget and you could end up damaging your bike – and forking out a lot of money.

2. Don't forget your battery

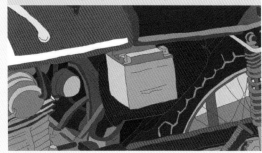

Remove the battery, disconnecting the earth (negative) terminal first. Examine the fluid level and, if necessary (or possible – you can't do this with sealed batteries), top it up with distilled water (never tap). Also check the contacts aren't corroded. If you need to charge the battery, use the correct type of charger and loosen the filler plugs to allow expanding gas to escape. *Don't* smoke, as the gas given off is explosive. Finally, reconnect the battery and check all the connections. Fit the earth terminal last.

3. Don't ignore your brakes

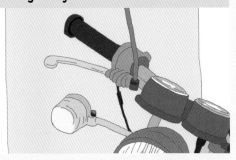

There are two types of brakes: mechanically operated and hydraulically operated. Ensure the cables of mechanically operated brakes are properly lubricated. On hydraulically operated brakes, check the brake fluid on the front and rear reservoirs – it should be between the minimum and maximum levels. Wear rubber gloves for this, or you're in for a rather unpleasant chemical peel. Next, with a torch, check the brake pads. Look for the amount of material left on the pads – you should have no less than 3mm (⅛in) on the pad.

4. Don't neglect your tyres

Using a depth gauge (available from all good motoring shops), check your tyres' tread. The minimum requirement for the grooves on the tread is 1mm (½in), but a thicker tread of 2–3mm (½2–⅛in) means your bike will stick to the road better. Then look for any lumps and bumps, any cuts or any sharp objects. Finally, check the pressure using a pressure gauge (buy your own, as the ones in petrol stations can be wildly inaccurate). Consult your owner's manual for the correct pressures. A damaged tyre should be replaced immediately.

Oil's Well

Oil is moisturiser for motorcycles. It lubricates the moving parts of the engine, gearbox and (where applicable) chain drive or shaft. It stops metal parts from rubbing against each other and also prevents rust and corrosion. And, rather like moisturisers, there are different oils for different parts. The quality is indicated by the API (American Petroleum Institute) grade. This is given in two letters: for engine oils, the first is always 'S'; the second ranges from 'A' (low quality) to 'H' (high). Make sure you use the correct grade of oil and keep it at the right level – check this with either a dipstick or sightglass. And don't be tempted by cheap oils – you'll only regret it in the long run.

CHECKING THE OIL

Do this as often as possible, in particular before a long journey. Check the oil when the engine is cold as the reading will be more accurate. Also ensure the bike is level and parked on its stand.

Your bike will have either a dipstick or a sightglass (basically, a small window).

With a dipstick:
Remove and wipe clean with a spare rag. Put the dipstick back in, remove it again, and look at the oil level. It should be between the maximum and minimum levels.

With a sightglass:
Wipe the sightglass clean. Again, the level should be between maximum and minimum.

CHANGING THE OIL

Change the engine oil at regular intervals – check your manufacturer's handbook for more information plus precise details on how to change the oil in your machine. Again, ensure the bike is standing upright on level ground. Make sure the old oil is hot when it's drained as this will remove any sediment. When changing the oil, also remember to change the filter at the same time. If you spill any on your hands, wash it off immediately.

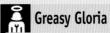
CHANGING THE GEARBOX OIL

Gearboxes are separate on all two-stroke engines and some four-stroke. Change the oil in accordance with your manufacturer's recommendations – once a year is usual. First drain the oil (easiest when the engine is warm) using the drain plug – check your handbook to ensure you are doing this correctly. Pour the old oil into a container. Replace with new oil using a funnel.

OILING THE DRIVE MECHANISM

Oils for the chain drive

Your bike will either have a chain drive or shaft drive. Rather like a bicycle chain, a motorcycle chain requires regular lubrication – use a special chain lubricant for this. Ride the bike before applying lubricant as it is better to lubricate a warm chain.

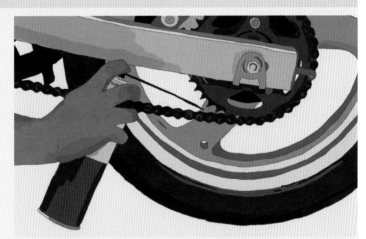

Oils for the shaft drive

With shaft drives, there will be a separate oil supply on the hub (centre) of the rear wheel. When checking the level, make sure the bike is in an upright position. Consult your manufacturer's handbook to ensure you use the correct oil.

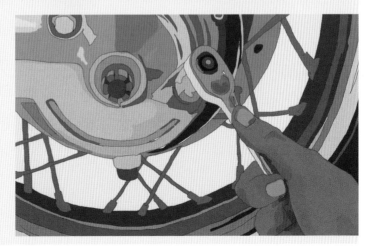

Braking Point

Your brakes are crucial: if you need to make an emergency stop, they must be in tip-top condition. Otherwise, quite frankly, you're in trouble. Show them a little TLC and they'll do you proud. Likewise, neglect your clutch and you'll start having problems changing gear. Read on for a brief guide to basic brake and clutch maintenance and repairs that you can do at home.

What is the brake shoe or pad?

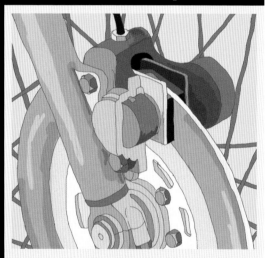

This is what rubs against the brake disc or drum to stop the machine. Because of all the friction involved, the shoes or pads suffer a lot of wear. They should be at least 3mm (⅛in) thick; any less, and replace them immediately, and always replace both, not just the one. Look at your manual on how to do this – it's a pretty basic exercise.

Also check for any leaks from oil or hydraulic fluid as this could decrease your bike's braking ability. As an oily brake pad or shoe is hard to clean properly, your best bet is to replace it immediately. And sort out the leak.

BRAKE MAINTENANCE

There are two types, disc and drum, and these can be either . . .

Hydraulically operated
Check the brake fluid levels regularly (top up using fluid from a fresh, unopened container) and the joints for any leaks. Leaks are bad news: not only will the brake fluid escape, but air could also get in. This can cause the brakes to become spongy when you squeeze the levers. Change the fluid every two to three years. Also make sure the flexible hoses aren't damaged in any way. And check brake pads and shoes for wear; replace regularly.

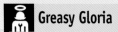

Greasy Gloria

Approximately every two years, renew the hydraulic fluid and check the various rubber bits of your brake system – you want them to be as effective as possible. If you need to change any of the rubber hoses, see a mechanic. Likewise, if you're experiencing any brake problems whatsoever, seek professional help immediately.

Mechanically operated

Adjust the brakes on a regular basis. Do this by shortening the length of the rod using a screw adjuster, remembering to leave sufficient free play. After any adjustments, always ensure that the brake light is still working. Make sure the pivots and cables are well lubricated with a spray lube. Again, check brake pads and shoes for wear and replace regularly.

CLUTCH MAINTENANCE

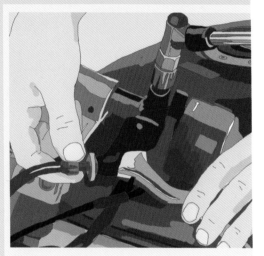

There are two types . . .

Hydraulically operated

As with brakes, check the fluid level regularly and check any couplings and joints for leaks. Also make sure the flexible hoses aren't damaged in any way.

Cable operated

Check the lever is working correctly and look out for any fraying cables. Also keep well-lubricated.

Suspension and Steering

The suspension system consists of the parts of the bike that join the wheel to the frame. It cushions both you and your bike from any bumps in the road – your backside would be sore without it. The front suspension consists of the front forks – below these are the wheel bearings; above are the steering bearings and handlebars. The rear suspension is made up chiefly of the shock absorbers. Steering is all about control: how the rider manoeuvres the machine. As with suspension, the front forks are key.

SUSPEND YOUR BELIEF

Maintenance of the suspension system consists of lubricating the bearings and checking for general wear and tear in the forks.

To do this: push down on the machine and watch the shock absorbers – there should be no bounce when the bike returns to its original height. If there is bounce, seek professional help. Also check the front forks and shock absorbers for oil leaks – this could make the bike difficult to control. Remember that you may have to alter your suspension if carrying an especially heavy load or a passenger.

STEER CLEAR

The steering head bearings above the front forks allow smooth steering movement. Check them regularly for wear and correct adjustment.

To do this: get someone to help you lift the bike or place the bike on bricks, then hold the front wheel off the ground. Try to move the forks backwards and forwards. Any problems and contact a mechanic. Also remember to check the handlebars – they should move freely as well.

You'll also need to check your wheel bearings and swingarm bearings. To examine the wheel bearings, enlist help to lift the wheel from the ground and rotate it, moving it around. If it seems wobbly, the bearings need replacing – get a professional mechanic to do this. The swingarm is the device that connects the rear wheel to the rest of the bike. Again, lift the rear wheel off the ground and push it from side to side. If there's any movement, the bearings should be replaced.

Electric Dreams

Bet you never thought you'd be dealing with your electrics. But maintaining your bike's electrical system – as opposed to repairing it, which in general we don't recommend – really isn't that hard. The system consists of the battery, generator, lights and horn. All should be checked regularly – see below for details. Any problems and consult a mechanic.

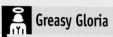
BATTERY AND LIGHTS

The battery powers the lights, horn and other electrical accessories, as well as providing power for the spark that ignites the engine.

Most batteries are sealed and require no maintenance. If the battery's not sealed, check that the plates in each cell (there are usually either three or six; each cell has two sets of metal plates) are sufficiently covered with fluid (a mixture of sulphuric acid and distilled water). Be very careful not to spill this on your skin – it will burn. If need be, top up the fluid with distilled water (never tap). Always keep the terminals and top of the battery clean and lubricate the terminals with some petroleum jelly to prevent corrosion. If you make lots of short trips with the lights on, you may need to recharge your battery from time to time.

It is a legal requirement that the lights and horn are fully functioning.

The lights include the front and rear lamps, brake lights, hazard lights and indicators. Check all these every time you set off. If one of the lights fails, check the fuse – the best way to do this is to replace it with a new one. All lights must be clean and show a steady beam. Always carry spare bulbs when you ride.

Indicators must flash between one and two times per second.

Also check the horn, although not during unsociable hours – otherwise, you'll have a neighbourhood riot on your hands.

Wheel Meet Again

The wheels and tyres have a lot to cope with, especially since this is your only direct contact with the road. They affect both your safety and your motorcycle handling, so tyre pressure and condition must be absolutely perfect. Although removing a wheel and changing a tyre is a job best left to the professionals, maintaining these parts of your bike is easy – and obvious.

WHEEL MAINTENANCE

- Check the alignment of the front and rear wheel. To do this: place a straight piece of wood along the length of the bike. Both wheels should be in line. If you adjust the wheel, you must adjust the chain tension at the same time.

- You must check that the wheels run 'true'. To do this: spin each wheel around while elevated off the ground. Check for any buckling or general wonkiness.

- Also check for damage – cracks, broken spokes, and so forth.

- Make sure the nuts and bolts are sufficiently tight.

- Have your wheels balanced regularly by a qualified mechanic or dealer.

 **Greasy Gloria**

Take care of your tyres because they really do take care of you – a puncture is no fun at all and a real hassle to get fixed. Braking or accelerating too hard will wear your tyres down quicker than usual, as will other factors such as defective forks and misaligned wheels. If you keep your riding steady and your eyes open for defects, you should get plenty of miles out of your rubber.

TYRE MAINTENANCE

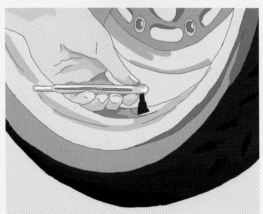

- Tyres are either tubed or tubeless.

- Check them regularly for cuts and for any debris stuck in them.

- Their condition is of the utmost importance. They are legally required to have a minimum tread of at least 1mm ($\frac{1}{25}$in). They also can't have a cut longer than 25mm (1in) or 10 per cent of the width of the tyre and can't have any exposed ply or cord. There must be no cuts or bulges in the sidewalls. If you find any damage, replace them immediately. Otherwise your handling will be impaired.

- If you get a puncture, don't brake sharply. Instead, close the throttle and stop at a gradual pace at the side of the road. Repair, or ideally replace, the tyre immediately.

- When replacing a tyre, make sure you buy the tyre recommended by your manufacturer. Some bikes have different front and rear tyres – consult your handbook for more details. You should also ensure that when your tyre is fitted, the tyre rotation indicators point in the right direction.

- Tyres must also be correctly inflated. Check the tyre pressure weekly when the tyres are cold; consult your manual for the correct pressure. Use your own pressure gauge as ones found in petrol stations can be very inaccurate. Remember to increase the pressure when carrying a heavy load or a passenger.

- If you need to inflate them, use a foot pump to add air. Make sure that you use your own gauge – as opposed to the one attached to the pump – to recheck the pressure, as again this will be more accurate.

- But what if your gauge *isn't* that accurate? Find out by taking your gauge to a specialist tyre shop and comparing it to their gauge. That way you'll always have utter faith in its reliability.

Beauty Therapy for Bikes

If motorcycle maintenance is a science, then keeping it clean is an art form. There are endless debates among riders about what is best for bikes – and certainly enough products on the market. But the one thing all riders agree on is that it is imperative to keep your machine spic and span – otherwise, it will lose its value. And you'll lose your self-esteem. Be proud of your bike.

Cleaning kit

- SOFT BRUSHES TO PROTECT THE PAINTWORK

- SPONGE

- CHAMOIS LEATHER

- A SPARE RAG

- VARIOUS BIKE WASHES/POLISHES INCLUDING A TAR REMOVER, WAX AND MOTORCYCLE SHAMPOO

WASHING AND WAXING

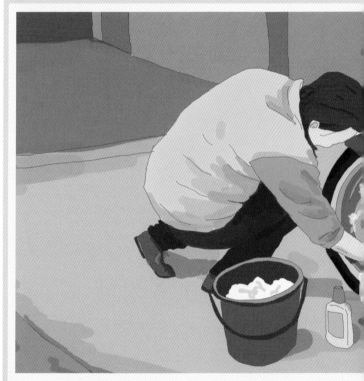

1 Wash the entire bike with motorcycle shampoo, a sponge and plenty of hot water. Rinse off with a hose, if possible.

2 Wash the bike again, this time using the soft brushes to remove dirt from any hard-to-reach places.

3 Rinse and then dry with a chamois leather. You can also use a leafblower (what gardeners use to clear leaves) for fast drying.

4 The frame may still be streaky from the shampoo. If so, make it gleam again with some bike polish.

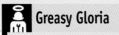

Greasy Gloria

Insects! The plague of many a motorcyclist. When cleaning your bike, pay special attention to rubbing away any bugs – fingernails are good for this (although it's not necessarily good for the fingernails). For an insect-splattered windscreen, try covering it with a hot, wet towel for 20 minutes to soften the dry bugs, then wipe off.

RUST AND DENTS

Rust should be tackled as soon as it's discovered.

Scrape it with a wire brush; follow this with emery paper. Then use a proprietary rust-killing chemical treatment, available from all good bike shops. Touch up the damaged area with undercoat and a topcoat (in either brush or aerosol form) that matches the colour of your bike. Make sure you get the exact shade.

Small dents may be lightly tapped out using a hammer covered in a cloth. However, it's best to deal with dents professionally – otherwise it's very easy to make things a whole lot worse.

Scratches are easier to deal with. If you find a scratch, clean round it with water, then paint over using touch-up paint. Do this very meticulously, brushing in the same direction. Wait a few days for everything to settle, then rub the area with a polishing compound to blend the new paint in.

5 Alternatively, use a wax – this will protect the metal parts from the ravages of road use (particularly salt on the roads in winter) and the weather. Any good bike shop will have a plethora of waxes on sale. Some are used after shampoo; others are all-in-ones: simply wash your bike, rinse, then buff with a chamois leather to produce a sheen.

6 Many bikers swear by the effectiveness of a jet-spray wash for a really thorough clean, but if you choose this method, use it carefully and sparingly. Jet sprays are powerful beasts that can strip a bike of its paint and indeed cause a great deal of damage. If using a jet spray, also remember to protect your bearings, chain and electrical system.

Troubleshooting Q&A

Don't have your mechanic on speed dial the second something goes wrong. By adopting a methodical approach – and that *doesn't* mean disassembling your machine bit by bit – most motorcycle problems can be swiftly solved. The reason your bike won't start, for instance, could be something as simple as running out of fuel. Below are the most common problems, the causes and some possible solutions.

Problem	Cause & Solution
✖ **No instrument lights** You turn the ignition key but the instrument lights don't come on.	✓ **Battery** It could be that your battery's flat. Or it might be a loose connection. Check the battery. If everything seems fine, recharge it.
✖ **Kick-start problems** On a bike with a kick-starter, you turn the key, the instrument lights come on but the bike won't start when you kick-start it.	✓ **Spark plugs** This could be down to dirty spark plugs. Your best bet, then, is to call a mechanic.
✖ **Bike runs poorly** The bike will actually start, but it feels jittery when it runs.	✓ **Carburettor** Check the air filter isn't clogged and the carburettor is in good nick. If you're still having a bumpy ride, visit a mechanic.
✖ **Spongy brakes** The brakes feel spongy and aren't working as sharply as they should.	✓ **Brake fluid and pads** Check the brake fluid: is it leaking? Is it at the correct level? Also examine the pads for wear. If the problem persists, visit a mechanic.
✖ **Uncomfortable ride** Your ride feels uncomfortable, particularly when going over bumps and potholes.	✓ **Suspension** There's something wrong with your suspension. Check by pressing down on the bike; if it bounces back up, there's trouble. Seek professional help.

Problem	Cause & Solution
✖ **Steering feels loose**	✓ **Forks and shocks**
The steering isn't as precise as usual and you feel as though you may lose control.	Check the front forks and shock absorbers for oil leaks. If your machine is still difficult to control, visit a mechanic.
✖ **Electrical failure**	✓ **Battery**
The lights won't go on and the horn's not working.	Blame your battery. Check the cell plates are sufficiently covered with fluid and recharge the battery. Still no joy? Visit a mechanic.
✖ **Excessive tyre wear**	✓ **Brakes**
Your tyres are wearing down at a faster rate than normal.	You may be using the front brake too much or it could be because you're regularly carrying an uneven load. Adjust your riding accordingly.
✖ **Tyre pressure loss**	✓ **Tyres**
Your tyres seem to be losing pressure much faster than normal.	Check your tyre for a possible slow puncture. Or have you considered the weather? The pressure falls faster as the temperature drops.
✖ **Wheels seem misaligned**	✓ **Wheels**
Your wheels don't appear to be running true and the front and rear are no longer aligned.	If you feel confident adjusting the wheels, remember to also alter the chain tension. But really, this is a job for a professional.

Ready, Steady . . . Go! The Ten-minute Road Check

Do this as often as possible – it's best to know if something's wrong before setting out. Any problems, and flip back through this book for possible solutions.

1   **FLUIDS:** Check the following and, if necessary, top up: the engine oil, the brake fluid, and the battery (where applicable). With a liquid-cooled engine, inspect the coolant level.

2   **FIDDLY BITS:** Make sure every visible nut and bolt is tight.

3   **CHAIN:** Check for correct tension and adequate lubrication. Also make sure there are no abnormalities – eg, kinks.

4   **WHEELS AND TYRES:** Do a quick recce for any cuts and debris, and monitor the general wear and state of the tread. Make sure the tyres are inflated to the correct pressure. Do a visual check every time you start a journey.

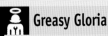
Greasy Gloria

Savvy motorcyclists know that your tyres need more than a cursory check. If they seem to be wearing quicker than usual, you may be using your front brake too much or regularly carrying an uneven load. So stop it! As for punctures, well you can get one tyre patched up, but two? Forget it. Don't risk your riding and buy a new tyre instead.

MIRRORS: Check that they're properly secured and look for any cracks. **5**

LIGHTS: The front and rear lights, brake lights, hazard lights and indicators must all be working. Replace any dead bulbs immediately. **6**

HORN: Check it's hooting properly. **7**

SUSPENSION: Check for sufficient lubrication on the bearings of both the front and rear suspension. Don't forget the shock absorbers: push down on your bike and watch its response. If it bounces back up, you're in trouble. Get to a mechanic. **8**

BRAKES: Test by squeezing the levers before setting off – your brakes must be absolutely perfect. If there are any problems, don't even think about riding – visit a mechanic immediately. Also check that the brake pads or shoes aren't worn, and that the brake fluid level is satisfactory. **9**

Road Sense: Hear Me Roar

Riding a motorcycle is unique: you grip and control it with your whole body, moving your weight around accordingly when making turns. It requires skill, confidence and care – this is not a pushbike; you are handling a potentially lethal weapon. Novices should be especially careful as the highest proportion of deaths is among newly qualified riders. Enough of the scaremongering. Here are pointers to bear in mind when riding . . .

Defensive riding

Want to be queen on the road? You'll need to polish up on your defensive and assertive riding skills first. Defensive riding means being aware of what's going on around you at all times, and anticipating the road ahead. There are several different factors you should consider, such as the weather, the traffic flow and the quality of light.

You must also be in a stable frame of mind: don't ride when angry, off-colour, distracted or drunk. You want to be in control at all times.

To anticipate the worst-case scenario, learn to read the road ahead. Is that car likely to turn without indicating? Is that bus stopping? The state of the road surface is also of utmost importance to motorcyclists. Watch out for any different colours – it could be oil or a diesel spill – and avoid them.

Assertive riding

Assertive riding is making others aware of you. Your position in the road should be wherever you're most visible to any passing car. Where possible, keep to the centre of the road. Always indicate before making any movements.

A good biker will be constantly on the lookout for safe 'gaps' in the traffic – you can use your manoeuvrability to exploit them. Don't ride up close behind another vehicle: think of the two-second rule. And remember to ride with your headlight on dipped beam at all times – even in bright sunlight. You really want everyone else on the road to see you.

Road rage

Our best tip? Avoid it! Be a courteous rider and don't offend other road users. Signal clearly, keep to the speed limits and keep your distance behind another vehicle.

If a situation occurs, try to defuse it as quickly as possible. If you feel you have done something wrong, acknowledge your mistake to the other road user. However, if you're the one getting into a tizzy, take a deep breath and put the situation into context. Become utterly emotionless. Don't take someone else's bad driving personally.

Safety and security

After all the maintenance and polishing you've been doing, you don't want to lose your bike, do you? Wherever possible, park it in a secure car park or on a busy street; at night, aim for a well-lit, busy area. Don't leave anything with your bike – this includes your helmet.

Invest in additional devices as well as your steering lock – consider splashing out on a heavy-duty chain lock or U-lock. The super-cautious can even get an alarm fitted. A Vehicle Identification Number is another good idea: if your stolen bike is found, this can help the police trace you.

Motorway riding

Before embarking on a motorway journey, make sure your motorcycle is safe and in good condition. Pay special attention to your tyres, lights and indicators, ensure your brakes are super-sharp and your steering ability perfect. You will also need to be very visible – you really want everyone to see you – so wear bright, reflective clothing. Make sure any load you are carrying is secure.

And don't forget to check your fuel, oil and water. Service stations may not be as frequent as you hope.

Greasy Gloria

Before riding anywhere, consider Gloria's golden rules to making your journey a whole lot easier and more enjoyable.

• Carry out regular maintenance checks (see pages 90–91).

• As much as possible, plan your route before setting off. This way your mind will be fully focused on the road.

• Be prepared: always carry essential kit (see page 73).

Carrying a Load

Want to get your shopping home in one piece? Fancy taking a bit of luggage away on holiday? A couple of tote bags just won't do. What you'll need is a specially designed carrier for your motorcycle that you can firmly attach to your bike. But that's not all: you may also have to adjust your tyres and even your driving when carrying a load. Not that simple, is it?

Carrier types

Panniers

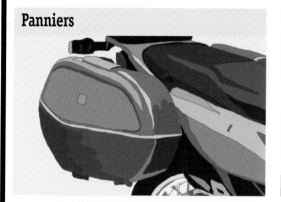

Come in two styles – rigidly fixed or throw-over saddle, both of which are self-explanatory. Choose one made of a heavy-duty material that can withstand the elements. And make sure you load each side evenly – you don't want to topple over.

Top box

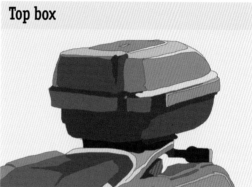

This is fixed to a rack behind the seat. Again, be careful about the load – anything too heavy concentrated in a specific area (in this case, the rear) will cause problems.

Tank bag

The best way to carry heavy loads. Fix this on top of your fuel tank, but make sure it doesn't interfere with your steering.

Luggage rack

Attaches luggage to the rear of the machine. The same rules apply – make sure your load is evenly distributed and securely fastened to the rack.

Greasy Gloria

Carrying a load isn't as simple as it sounds. You may have to adjust your riding as well as your tyres . . .

- Get yourself accustomed to the new weight before embarking on a long journey. It's a good idea to go on a practice run.

- Remember your tyres: you may need to inflate them. Check out your bike manual for the recommended pressure. You may also need to adjust your suspension and lights.

- This point can't be overemphasised: your luggage must be evenly

distributed; otherwise, it may affect the handling of the machine. Also ensure it is securely fixed – watch out for hanging straps that could obscure the wheels – and well positioned.

- When parking your bike, lock your luggage. Better still, take it with you.

Towing a trailer

THIS IS FOR WHEN YOU HAVE A LOT OF GEAR TO CARRY – BUT NOT A PASSENGER; A TRAILER IS NOT THE SAME AS A SIDECAR. BEAR THE FOLLOWING IN MIND . . .

- To tow a trailer, your bike must have an engine capacity of more than 125cc.

- The best trailers have solid frames, preferably made from hand-laid fibre glass (this will be very strong). You should also look for a trailer that is as light as possible – the less it weighs empty, the more you can carry. Also think about the width – if you're overtaking something, you want your trailer to clear it as well.

- Speak to your dealer about the legalities of a trailer – the maximum size allowed for your bike, the maximum weight, and the distance required between the rear of your machine and

the rear of the trailer. Also ask the dealer about any speed restrictions that may apply.

- The same rules apply with a trailer as with a load in general: you may need to adjust your tyres and your driving. Your stopping distance may also be affected.

- Remember to carry an adequate tool kit to fix any problems while on the road.

- Most importantly, never forget your trailer is there. Sounds silly, but it has been known!

Carrying a Passenger

All aboard, please! Actually, you can't carry too many people. You can feasibly carry one passenger pillion; possibly two child-sized ones in a sidecar. Yet carrying a passenger is one of the most difficult riding skills to master. Read on for some advice on what to do . . .

- You can only carry a pillion passenger once you have a full motorcycle licence and have passed your practical motorcycle test.

- If carrying a passenger, you are legally required to make sure you have footrests and an adequate passenger seat.

- For a pillion passenger, you need the right sort of bike with a proper seat. In general, touring bikes are best for this.

- Tell your passenger exactly what to do before you set off. Here's a checklist of things to remember:

  Provide them with a helmet.

  Tell them exactly where to put their feet.

A note on sidecars

Sidecars may have a whiff of Toad of Toad Hall about them, but they can be very handy when carrying an extra passenger or indeed an extra-heavy load – with the latter, sidecars are especially good.

- Ask your dealer if your machine is suitable for a sidecar – not all bikes are. If your motorcycle can take a sidecar, think about price (they are expensive) and colour (it's best to get one that can match your bike, although many can be painted).

- Again, you must adapt your driving. On bends in particular, remember to take special precautions as the sidecar must be steered by pushing/pulling the handlebar.

- Your braking will be affected. The extra weight may make it more difficult to stop.

- If in doubt, practise riding before setting out on a trip.

Show them how to sit – they can either hold your waist or hold the passenger grab-handle.

Demonstrate how to lean into bends with you.

Don't ask your passenger to look behind or ahead, or signal for you.

Tell your passenger to sit as still as possible. Wrigglers will make your ride even more troublesome.

- Think about clothes. Your passenger should be wearing a similar outfit to your own – warm, waterproof, protective clothing; bright and reflective if riding at night.

- As well as kitting themselves out in bright, waterproof gear, your passenger must also wear suitable clothes for riding. So no floaty scarves. If in doubt, remember what happened to Isadora Duncan.

- Adjust your riding technique. Go on a practice run with a passenger, taking it slowly at first. Your balance will be different, especially when riding at lower speeds. Your stopping distance will also be affected.

- Your tyres may need adjusting – look at your machine's manual for the recommended pressures. Check the manual to see if you need to adjust the pre-load on the rear shock absorbers, or move your rear light.

- Check that your combined weight does not exceed the carrying capacity recommended by your manufacturer.

- You can carry children pillion if they can properly reach the footrests and handrails. However, it is not recommended.

- Most importantly, before setting off, make sure that your passenger is comfortable with the bike and relaxed about going pillion.

- And if you're passenger-free, remember that you can still utilise the passenger seat for luggage secured with bungee cords.

All-Weather Driving: How To Be a Weather Girl

Riding a bike leaves you very exposed to the elements. Of course you always hope for glorious sunshine – but in many countries that's simply a pipe dream. Before setting out, not only must you think carefully about wearing the correct clothing for the weather conditions, but you must also remember to adapt your riding technique. For a biker, the smallest changes in road surface – for instance, a patch of wet leaves or some light snow – can be critical. So be prepared. And make sure your bike is in tip-top condition.

Fog

Let's start with the worst. Fog is arguably the most dangerous condition to ride in: if at all possible, avoid. Not only is your visibility affected, but other road users will also have difficulty seeing you. Wear bright clothes and keep your headlight on dipped beam. Don't use the main beam as it could dazzle other drivers as well as you since the fog reflects the light.

Your visor or goggles will also pose a problem as they can mist up on both the outside and inside. Carry a cloth with you at all times and if misting occurs, pull over and wipe frequently. If you're riding in freezing fog, the mist on your goggles or visor can actually freeze over. Stop immediately and de-ice them.

Wind

Strong winds mean high fuel consumption and in extreme conditions can even cause you to topple over. Bikes are especially exposed when passing gaps in hedges or buildings, or riding on an exposed road. Try and ride in the middle of the lane – this will give you more room to manoeuvre if you start swaying. Remember to alter riding position too. Grip the bike with your lower body while allowing your upper body to move with the wind.

Greasy Gloria

Whatever the weather, always carry a clean cloth with you – you never know when your visor or goggles will need a quick wipe. If riding in foggy conditions, consider splashing out on a helmet with air vents or one of the anti-fog products now on the market. It pays to be as cautious as possible.

Snow

Again, if it can be avoided, don't ride in snow. Drive slowly and carefully, make sure your visor or goggles remain clear, and regularly remove any snow from the headlight and indicators. And keep snuggled up. If you become too cold, your concentration will waver – it's worth investing in good-quality clothing to keep warm. Pay particular attention to your hands and feet.

In addition, don't forget to check the coolant (the mixture of anti-freeze and water in the engine) more regularly in cold weather.

Rain

As with all bad weather conditions, rain can affect your ability to see clearly. Any rain on your visor or goggles means you should stop immediately and demist. You will also need to think about your

clothes. Keeping dry is of the utmost importance, otherwise your concentration will be affected.

Because of reduced tyre grip on a wet road, particularly if rain follows a prolonged dry spell (because this will loosen all the oil and other gunge on the surface), you will need to allow longer for stopping. Likewise, your brakes are likely to be less effective. Be specially aware of wet leaves, rain on metal drain covers, and painted road markings – these can be extra slippery. The solution to all this? Keep your speed down.

Ice

Established ice is bad enough; more slippery still is when the ice is about to freeze or thaw. Black ice is the name given to almost invisible ice patches on a normally good road surface. If the road looks wet but your tyres aren't acting the way they would normally with rain, chances are it's black ice, which is a biker's biggest enemy. Ride slowly. Better still, don't ride at all.

Winterising your bike

All sounds very hazardous, doesn't it? So it's not really surprising that many bikers are fair-weather riders and choose to pack their bike away for the winter months. But you can't simply put it in a garage and forget about it. Here are some basic steps on how to winterise your machine …

- Firstly, check the motorbike thoroughly for any mechanical problems.

- Change the engine oil and filter.

- Thoroughly clean and wax the bike.

- Cover with a tailor-made bike sheet or old blanket.

- Leave in a locked garage, preferably one that is warm.

- Ensure that the registration papers are kept separately from the bike in case it is stolen.

Roadside Situations: If It All Goes Wrong . . .

Statistically, you are most likely to have a motorcycle accident less than 10km (6⅕ miles) from your home and in the first 12 minutes of your ride. But of course you can't predict an accident or, indeed, a breakdown. Read on to find out what to do if the unexpected happens.

If your bike breaks down:
This is why you should always travel with a basic tool kit . . .

1 Pull over and stop immediately. Make sure you park away from any oncoming traffic.

2. Isolate and diagnose the problem. Be honest, now – can you solve it? If not, call a vehicle rescue organisation (hopefully with the mobile phone you should always carry with you).

3 There is a real sense of camaraderie among the biking community, so if you're lucky, a white knight will come to your rescue. This works both ways: if you spot someone who has broken down, stop and offer your services. Think of it as biking karma.

If you find yourself at the scene of an accident:
1 Further collisions may happen, so warn other traffic by switching on your hazard lights or – if not available – other lights; or place a warning triangle in the road.

2 Call the emergency services if necessary.

3 Manage any injured parties in the following way: move injured people away from the vehicle/s and into a safe place BUT don't move people unnecessarily. Don't move people who are

If someone is injured, remember:

A Airways must be cleared of any obstruction.

B Breathing must be maintained. If there is no breathing, attempt mouth-to-mouth resuscitation.

C Blood circulation must be maintained and any bleeding stopped with a firm pressure using clean material if possible.

trapped inside a vehicle unless they're in danger (from fire, for instance). If you're dealing with a biker, don't remove their helmet.

4 If you see an accident and there are already enough people involved, carry on – you may be more of a hindrance than a help.

If you are involved in a road accident:
1 You MUST stop. As before, warn other traffic to prevent further collisions by switching on hazard lights or placing a warning triangle in the road.

2 Switch off the engine.

3 If someone is injured, call the emergency services.

4 Call the police if someone is hurt, if you've damaged someone's property but you can't find them to tell them, if the road is blocked with debris, or if someone leaves the scene of the accident without exchanging details.

5 Get the names, addresses and phone numbers (avoid mobiles) of any witnesses. Also get the name, address and phone number of the other party as well as their insurance details – check that he/she is the owner of the vehicle.

6 Note down the make, model, colour and registration number of the other vehicle/s involved. Also make a note of the damage sustained. Jot down any other pertinent details: weather conditions, road conditions, what everyone involved said, whether the other party's lights/indicators were on, and so forth.

7 Make a note of the exact location of the collision and how it happened. It can help to draw a map while the situation is still clear in your mind or, if you have a camera, take photos.

8 Be nice to the other party, even if they're acting like a monster. But do not discuss liability – and under no circumstances admit it.

Greasy Gloria

In case of an emergency or accident, always carry a pen and paper with you – to jot down any names/details – and a mobile phone. It's also wise to invest in a small fire extinguisher.

Learn the Lingo

This book is all about basic maintenance. So don't be embarrassed if you need to see a mechanic – in some cases (for example, when getting your wheels balanced) you will have no choice. As with all things vehicular, workshops and dealerships can be testosterone-fuelled environments, where it's easy to feel intimidated. Read on for some tips on how to handle the professionals, and a little more about all the new terminology you'll need to know (fairings, anyone?). Gen up, go in with your head held high, and refuse to be bullied.

Dealing with the professionals

As is always the case when dealing with specialists, try and use a mechanic recommended by a friend. If this isn't a possibility, shop around for the best quote. Remember that you shouldn't be charged for the initial examination. And ask for a written quotation before work gets started.

Another tip: do your homework. Find out the price of any parts that need replacing – call your motorcycle manufacturer if necessary to ask the recommended retail price. This way you'll know if you're paying a fair price for the repairs. It's also worth asking the mechanic to return the old parts to you when your bike has been repaired – so you can be sure you're actually getting new parts. Although they could, admittedly, simply try giving you any old bit of junk.

On payment, go through the bill carefully. Make sure it is itemised and question any additional costs immediately. Don't leave upset and return the following day – they could argue that when you left you were perfectly happy. Clear up any problems immediately.

Parlez-vous motorbike?

A BRIEF GLOSSARY OF TECHNICAL TERMS.

Allen key
A six-sided L-shaped slot-in tool that comes in a set of varying sizes; good for adjustments to recessed bolts.

Brake pads/shoes
Pads that touch the brake disks or drums when the brake lever is applied.

Bearings
Minimise friction between fixed and moving bike parts.

Carburettor
Part of the fuel system, this mixes the petrol with the air so it will ignite.

Choke
Alters the amount of air in the petrol/air mixture that the engine burns.

Cruiser
A style of bike with a low body and high handlebars (Harley-Davidson is the most famous example).

Cut-out switch
Ensure this is on before turning the ignition key.

Cylinder
The part of the engine where the petrol/air mixture is burned to provide power to drive the machine.

Dipstick
Device for checking oil levels.

Drive chain
The chain that channels the power from the engine to the rear wheel.

Fairings
Made from heavy-duty materials such as fibreglass, these protect the rider from the weather.

Four-stroke engine
Generally runs on unleaded fuel.

Handlebar muffs
Can be added to your bike to keep your hands warm and dry.

Ignition switch
On the instrument panel; turn your key here to get the bike going.

Kick-starter
What you stamp down on repeatedly until the engine starts.

Mileometer
On the instrument panel; shows you how many miles your bike has travelled.

Pannier
A holdall that fits on to the rear of the bike.

Rev
Short for revolutions. This is how the engine speed of a motorcycle is measured.

Sam Browne belt
A fluorescent reflective belt, necessary for driving in poor visibility.

Sightglass
Device for checking oil levels.

Speedometer
On the instrument panel; tells you your speed.

Steering head bearings
Two sets of ball bearings located above and below the frame's head tube. Necessary for smooth steering and control.

Throttle
Increases or decreases the engine's revs and therefore how fast you go.

Torque wrench
A specially designed wrench that makes a loud click when the exact amount of force required for the nut and bolt has been applied, preventing you from over- or under-tightening the joint.

Two-stroke engine
Runs on a mixture of petrol and oil.

Winterise
How to properly store your bike over the winter months if you're a fair-weather rider.

Driving Abroad: Foreign Bodies

Riding across India on an Enfield or doing Route 66 on a Harley is the sort of once-in-a-lifetime holiday people dream of. But if you're thinking of taking your bike abroad, there are certain factors you should bear in mind . . .

- Have a full service before setting out. If you get any new parts fitted, wait for them to settle down – this could take a few weeks.

- When riding abroad, always carry your driving licence. Many non-EU countries require an International Driving Permit (although you must take your other licence too). Check before you set out.

- You'll need other documentation as well. Always carry your Vehicle Registration Document and insurance documents. Third party insurance is compulsory in most countries.

- Carry a few more tools than normal – in fact, as many as you can hold. Always, always take your bike's handbook.

- In some countries it is a legal requirement to carry a spare set of bulbs and a first aid kit. Both are worth carrying anyway.

- Find out about the rules and regulations of the country you'll be travelling in before setting off.

- Remember to display your nationality on the back of your bike.

- Be especially careful if riding in a country where traffic drives on the opposite side of the road to that in your own country. Remember that your headlamp will no longer dip correctly. Attach a deflector triangle (from all good bike shops) to the light to redirect most of the glare.

- Make sure your luggage is securely positioned and that the weight is evenly distributed (see pages 94–95 for more details).

- Prepare, prepare, prepare. Plan the journey – don't take on more than you're capable of. Have plenty of breaks, especially if you're riding at dusk when accidents are most likely to occur, or in the early hours of the morning.

- Bon voyage!

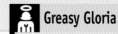 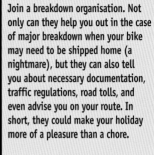

Greasy Gloria

Join a breakdown organisation. Not only can they help you out in the case of major breakdown when your bike may need to be shipped home (a nightmare), but they can also tell you about necessary documentation, traffic regulations, road tolls, and even advise you on your route. In short, they could make your holiday more of a pleasure than a chore.

Pedal Power

Rear wheel:
Includes tyre, tube and spokes.

Gearing system:
To help you whatever the road or weather.

Saddle:
Think comfort, think the specially designed women's saddle.

Chain:
Transforms your pedalling power into bike power.

'Nothing since has equalled that birdlike freedom.'
NOVELIST ELIZABETH BOWEN (1899–1973) ON OWNING HER FIRST BIKE

Pedal:
And these will help harness
that power.

Handlebars:
Different types include drop
(pictured), flat and riser.

Front wheel:
Needs care and attention –
or you'll be going nowhere.

Brakes:
Without fail, check these
before setting off.

What Bike Should I Buy?

Bikes are a cheap, environmentally friendly way to travel, but buying the right one is not without its complications. Not all cycles are the same. Some even have curly handlebars and chunky tyres. So what type of bike should you go for? Read on to find the right vehicle for you and your lifestyle.

CYCLE SHOPPING

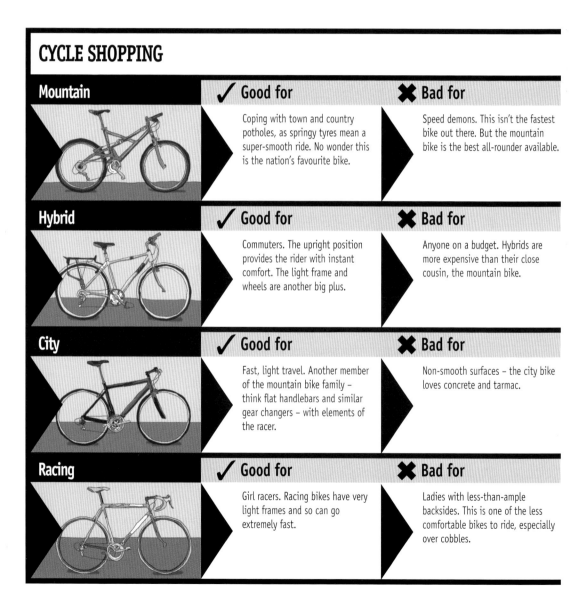

Mountain

✓ Good for

Coping with town and country potholes, as springy tyres mean a super-smooth ride. No wonder this is the nation's favourite bike.

✖ Bad for

Speed demons. This isn't the fastest bike out there. But the mountain bike is the best all-rounder available.

Hybrid

✓ Good for

Commuters. The upright position provides the rider with instant comfort. The light frame and wheels are another big plus.

✖ Bad for

Anyone on a budget. Hybrids are more expensive than their close cousin, the mountain bike.

City

✓ Good for

Fast, light travel. Another member of the mountain bike family – think flat handlebars and similar gear changers – with elements of the racer.

✖ Bad for

Non-smooth surfaces – the city bike loves concrete and tarmac.

Racing

✓ Good for

Girl racers. Racing bikes have very light frames and so can go extremely fast.

✖ Bad for

Ladies with less-than-ample backsides. This is one of the less comfortable bikes to ride, especially over cobbles.

CYCLE SHOPPING

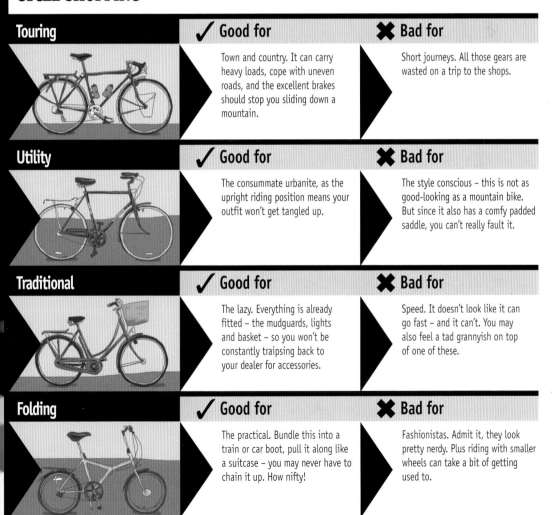

Touring

✓ Good for

Town and country. It can carry heavy loads, cope with uneven roads, and the excellent brakes should stop you sliding down a mountain.

✗ Bad for

Short journeys. All those gears are wasted on a trip to the shops.

Utility

✓ Good for

The consummate urbanite, as the upright riding position means your outfit won't get tangled up.

✗ Bad for

The style conscious – this is not as good-looking as a mountain bike. But since it also has a comfy padded saddle, you can't really fault it.

Traditional

✓ Good for

The lazy. Everything is already fitted – the mudguards, lights and basket – so you won't be constantly traipsing back to your dealer for accessories.

✗ Bad for

Speed. It doesn't look like it can go fast – and it can't. You may also feel a tad grannyish on top of one of these.

Folding

✓ Good for

The practical. Bundle this into a train or car boot, pull it along like a suitcase – you may never have to chain it up. How nifty!

✗ Bad for

Fashionistas. Admit it, they look pretty nerdy. Plus riding with smaller wheels can take a bit of getting used to.

Know Your Bike

Understanding Your Wheels

So you've deliberated, cogitated and are now the proud owner of the perfect bike. But there's still more to learn. Once bikes were made from steel and plastics – pretty basic stuff. Now it's NASA all the way, with lightweight materials such as carbon fibre and titanium used on aerodynamic bikes created by high-tech computer design.

And it doesn't stop there. Front and rear suspension is another advancement – this is now standard on many mountain bikes, allowing riders to navigate pretty much any sort of terrain. And then there are the gears: originally, three were the norm; now

1 **HANDLEBARS:** All you really need to know is that you have three options: drop (found on racers and some touring bikes), flat (found on roadsters, hybrids and utility bikes) and riser (again, a feature of utility as well as mountain bikes). What suits you is all down to personal preference.

2 **SADDLE:** Comfort is key. Saddles are available in a wide range of materials, shapes, sizes and padding. The only way to know what's right for you is to sit on as many as possible. Do consider gel-filled saddles, though, as the gel moulds round the rider's bum. Hey presto, a bespoke seat!

3 **BRAKING SYSTEM:** Cantilever and V-brakes squeeze the wheel rim (the part of the wheel closest to the tyre) to stop the bike. Hub-mounted brakes work in a similar way but at the hub (the centre of the wheel). Hydraulic brakes operate in a similar way to those on a car.

4 **GEARING SYSTEM:** Derailleur gears (pictured) are most common – as the gears change, the chain 'derails' from one sprocket to another. You can also get hub gears. These have a gearbox built into the hub (centre) of the rear wheel.

5 **WHEELS:** Consist of the tyre, tube, rim, spokes and hub. A good bike will have aluminium alloy wheel rims (the part of the wheel that touches the tyre), which are light and rust-free. Also look out for stainless steel spokes, as they're less likely to corrode.

some bikes can have 27 or more. Exhausting, no? Don't fret, though: the basic stuff to do with how the bike works – the pedalling, steering and braking – has remained the same since the days of the penny-farthing.

Still not know your tubes from your tyres? Can't distinguish your handlebars from your saddle? Here's a little more information on what exactly goes where.

Basic Bike Kit

Put those spike heels away. What you'll need, boring as it may sound, are sensible shoes, tight-fitting-yet-flexible clothes, and a helmet. If necessary and you want to arrive somewhere smart, carry a change of clothes in your backpack. Your bike could do with accessorising, too, otherwise it might feel left out. Here are some suggestions for equipment and clothing for all kinds of weather.

SHIRT	**CYCLING SHORTS**	**SHOES**	**FLEECE**	**CYCLING GLOVES**	**RAINY WEATHER GEAR**

| Day-glo colours, especially yellow, will get you noticed. | Not just a fashion relic from the 1980s. These will keep you cool and comfortable in warm weather. | You can buy cycling shoes designed for compatibility with pedals, but trainers are fine. | The best way to stay warm. Different levels of thickness mean different levels of insulation. | Usually fingerless with mesh backs and gel-filled palms. Crucial for cushioning during a fall. | The best gear is made from fabric that stops water getting in while allowing perspiration out. |

Helmet help

The vast majority of fatal bike accidents are caused by an injury to the head. Wearing a helmet is still not a legal must – but you'd be a fool to go without. In fact, nowadays, you're more likely to get funny looks if you're NOT wearing one. Here are some tips about what to look for:

LIGHTS	PANNIER	LOCK	MUDGUARDS

Cyclists are legally required to ride with a white light at the front and a red at the rear.	This is a holdall that fits onto a cycle rack, usually at the back of the bike. Good for heavy loads.	A heavy-duty D-lock will provide the best security for your bike.	Crucial in winter, unless you actually like the muddy look.

REFLECTORS	WATER BOTTLE	PUMP	MULTI-TOOL

Essential for night riding and a necessary backup for lights.	Because cycling can be thirsty work, especially in hot weather.	Ensure this fits your tyre valve type.	This very clever device contains spanners and Allen keys of several different sizes.

1 Choose a dealer with a wide selection. Helmets must reach certain safety standards. In the UK, the safest ones are those that have passed the Snell Foundation test.

2 A good-quality helmet should offer plenty of ventilation, with lots of air channels running from front to back.

3 The helmet should sit low on your brow, but high enough to allow clear vision upwards and sideways. A two-finger gap between eyebrows and helmet should be sufficient.

4 Is the fit correct? When the chinstrap is properly adjusted and fastened, you should not be able to move the helmet backwards and forwards with your hands.

5 Also consider a nape strap. If properly fitted (fractionally below the bulge in the skull), it should stop the helmet from slipping back.

6 Replace the helmet after every crash, however minor, and again after every two or three years. The inside foam won't stay supple forever.

Tool Box Essentials

A cycle tool kit is relatively simple – after all, bikes tend to be more reliable than something with an engine. That's not to say they don't have temperamental moments, though. So this is what you'll need when your bike's having an off day and needs some TLC at home.

Greasy Gloria

Don't leave home without...

Some tools are needed for basic maintenance at home, while others are crucial for any mid-ride dramas. Clever cyclists carry the following at all times:

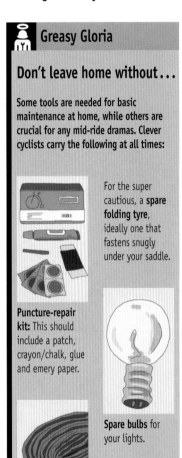

For the super cautious, a **spare folding tyre**, ideally one that fastens snugly under your saddle.

Puncture-repair kit: This should include a patch, crayon/chalk, glue and emery paper.

Spare bulbs for your lights.

A pump.

NB If you're touring, consider bringing as much of the tool kit as you can carry (see page 140).

A spare tube.

Whoa, there!

So you're kitted out, you've bought all the gear on the opposite page, and you're ready to go. Hold on a minute: there are certain rules to uphold when it comes to tools.

Don't be heavy handed

Your bike might look sturdy and robust but compared to most other vehicles, it is pretty weedy, especially if the frame is made from a lightweight material. So when it comes to maintenance and repairs, a light touch is required. This rule applies in particular to nuts and bolts – whatever you do, don't over-tighten them. Don't trust your own strength? Then invest in a torque wrench, a brilliant device that makes a loud clicking sound when the correct amount of force has been applied.

Spanner manners

There is a certain art form to using a spanner correctly. For a start, you should always turn the tool towards you. That way, not only do you have more control, you are also less likely to cause injury to yourself.

A process of trial and error should help you work out which implement is best for which part. As a rule of thumb, ring spanners or sockets are better than open-ended ones as they can actually grip the hexagonal nut or bolt in each one of the six corners. This means the nut or bolt is less likely to get damaged. However, you will occasionally need to use an open-ended spanner. Because it grips only two corners of the nut or bolt, this is a considerably trickier tool to handle. To minimise the likelihood of any damage, try steadying your hand on another part of the bike near to where you're working.

Sockets are perfect for when a nut is hidden away, for instance on the pedals. Gear mechs often use Phillips screws, so tackle these with a Phillips screwdriver. Finally, try to remember the order things come apart – maybe lay them carefully in sequence on a sheet of newspaper. This will make it a million times easier when it comes to reassembly.

Quality control

Blow the bank and buy the best tools. It will be worth it in the long run as they'll last longer, plus a cheap tool could damage your bike. Keep all your tools clean and free from rust – storing them in a specially designed box is ideal. Have a clean rag handy and wear plastic gloves – the ones used by medical students are ideal – as bike work can get messy, especially where greases are involved. You're ready now. Happy tinkering!

Head tool school

WHEN IT COMES TO A QUICK NIP AND TWEAK, BICYCLES DON'T REQUIRE THAT MUCH IN THE WAY OF APPARATUS. TO BE A HALFWAY DECENT AMATEUR MECHANIC, HOWEVER, YOU'LL NEED TO INVEST IN THE FOLLOWING . . .

OILS AND GREASES: An array of lubricants is necessary for cleaning and servicing (see pages 132–33 for more details).

PUMP: Make sure you buy one that fits your tyre valve type.

PLIERS: For pulling cables.

TOOTHBRUSH: Believe it or not, a tiny brush like this is the best way to clean your bike.

TYRE LEVERS: Essential for mending a puncture.

TORQUE WRENCH: This will make a loud click when the exact amount of force required for the nut or bolt has been applied.

SCREWDRIVERS: Flathead for adjusting gears, plus Phillips (sizes 1 and 2) for other jobs.

METRIC SPANNERS: Your set should include 8, 9, 10, 11mm sizes of both the box-end (ring) and the open-end types.

ALLEN KEYS: Essential for adjusting many components on a bike.

MULTI-TOOL: Useful for making quick, minor adjustments.

Cycle Science: Understanding How Your Bike Works

Before you get on to the matter of bicycle maintenance and repairs, you'll need to know how the darn thing actually works. Like most things in life, the mechanics of a bike aren't a great mystery; how it works is mostly down to common sense. And if you know how it works, it's easier to figure out what is wrong. The following is an elementary lesson in cycle science that should shed some light on how to maintain and repair your cycle, as well as eliminate any embarrassingly blank looks if you ever need to consult a mechanic.

The easy part

How do I move?

Well, dear rider, it's all down to you – with a little help from the pedals, the chain and the wheels. Basically, your muscle power is turned into mechanical power via the pedals, cranks (the bit connecting the pedals to the main frame) and chain (think of this as the heart of the bike). Which spins the wheel, which in turn propels the bike forwards. Suddenly, it all makes sense . . .

And when I stop?

It's thanks to the brakes. You squeeze the two brake levers connected to the brake cables; this immediately stops the wheels from spinning. When you brake, a brake pad presses against the wall of the wheel's rim. These brake pads are extremely important and must be checked regularly (see pages 120–21 for more details). The right brake lever controls the front wheel, the left the back. You'd be surprised how few people actually know this.

A bit more technical

How, exactly, do gears work?

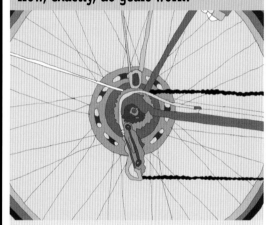

Gears are vital for safe riding whatever the terrain or weather. Low gears are for climbing hills, while high gears are for going back down again.

There are two types of gear: derailleur and hub. Derailleur gears derail the chain from one sprocket to another. They have a front mech, a metal 'cage' attached to the seat post that moves the chain between two or three chainrings, and a rear mech with up to ten sprockets. Hub gears have fewer speeds and are housed within a single rear hub. Both types operate via cables connected to the gear shifters on the handlebars or down frame.

At the back wheel, the smaller the sprocket, the higher the gear. The opposite is true for the chainwheel (the front sprocket attached to the right crank). Here the larger the chainring, the higher the gear.

A bit about the headset

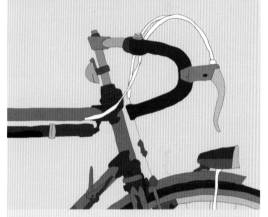

The headset consists of two sets of ball bearings located above and below the frame's head tube. On top of the tube are the stem and handlebars; below is the fork. The headset allows the handlebars, fork and stem to turn inside the head tube. This in turn ensures smooth steering.

The headset is the part of the bike most overlooked when it comes to maintenance and repairs, as many riders think a fault here would be blindingly obvious. This isn't necessarily the case. To find out more, turn to page 130.

Basic Maintenance and Repairs

The bicycle is officially the world's favourite vehicle: an estimated eight out of ten people worldwide own, or have access to, a bike. But do you think all these people have the first clue about what to do when they get a puncture? Or a loose chain? Of course not, but with the help of the following fourteen pages, you can be one of the practical few – and a woman, too! Bike repairs in general are not *too* tricky; they just require a little know-how and some common sense. The same goes for general maintenance. If you give your cycle the right amount of TLC, it will last you for the rest of your life. How's that for an investment?

Chore Chart: What to do when

WEEKLY:

- CHECK THE BRAKES. RIDE A FEW METRES THEN GIVE THEM A GOOD SQUEEZE – YOU SHOULD ONLY HAVE TO PULL HALFWAY DOWN FOR THEM TO PROPERLY WORK. IF THEY'RE NOT WORKING, DON'T USE THE BIKE.
- TYRES. CHECK PRESSURE AND GIVE THEM THE ONCE-OVER FOR STRAY DEBRIS (SUCH AS NAILS).
- WHEELS. MAKE SURE THE SPOKES AREN'T DAMAGED AND THAT THE WHEELS ARE 'TRUE' AND CORRECTLY ALIGNED.
- TEST THE LIGHTS.
- CHECK THE BELL.
- CHECK THE SADDLE IS TIGHT – THERE SHOULD BE NO MOVEMENT.
- GIVE THE BIKE A QUICK ALL-OVER WIPE WITH A CLOTH.

FORTNIGHTLY:

- MAKE SURE THE CHAIN IS OILED AND PROPERLY ADJUSTED.
- LOOK AT THE BRAKE PADS (THE PART OF THE BRAKE THAT TOUCHES THE WHEEL RIM WHEN THE BRAKE LEVER IS APPLIED). THERE SHOULD BE LOTS OF RUBBER LEFT AND AT LEAST 1MM ($\frac{1}{16}$IN) BETWEEN THE PAD AND THE RIM OF THE WHEEL.
- CHECK THE HEADSET FOR SMOOTH STEERING MOVEMENT, PAYING PARTICULAR ATTENTION TO ANY MOVEMENT BETWEEN THE FORKS (THE TUBE THAT ATTACHES YOUR HANDLEBARS TO YOUR WHEELS) AND THE FRAME. ANY PROBLEMS AND YOUR BIKE COULD BE DIFFICULT TO CONTROL.
- HOLD ONE PEDAL STILL AND TRY TO MOVE THE OTHER. IF THERE'S ANY MOVEMENT, YOU SHOULD TIGHTEN THE BOLTS.

MONTHLY:

- CHECK THE LUBRICATION ON THE BRAKES, HUBS, GEARS AND BEARINGS (DEVICES DESIGNED TO MINIMISE FRICTION OF MOTION BETWEEN FIXED AND MOVING BIKE PARTS). AS YOU MAY HAVE GATHERED BY NOW, THERE ARE A LOT OF MOVING PARTS ON A BICYCLE, AND A DROP OF OIL WILL GO A LONG WAY TO KEEP THEM MOVING SMOOTHLY.
- TIGHTEN ALL VISIBLE NUTS AND BOLTS SUCH AS THOSE ON YOUR RACKS, BRAKE LEVERS AND GEAR SHIFTERS.
- CHECK FOR ANY FRAYING BRAKE AND GEAR CABLES.
- GIVE YOUR BIKE A PROPER CLEAN USING LUBES AND DEGREASERS, BRUSHES AND SPONGES (SEE PAGES 132–33 FOR MORE DETAILS).

Greasy Gloria's No-Nos

1. Don't be Mrs Muscle

When loosening and tightening various bicycle parts with a spanner, be gentle. Bike bits are usually made of lightweight materials, which are strong but not super-robust. So when tightening or loosening nuts and bolts, you should be firm (otherwise they'll fall off), but not *too* firm. Also remember the clockwise/anticlockwise rule. Which is: tighten in a clockwise direction; loosen in an anticlockwise direction.

2. Don't forget to check your lights

Otherwise, you'll have the law to deal with. The law in many countries states that cyclists must ride with a white light at the front and a red at the rear. Those in the know also recommend a flashing light, using a Light Emitting Diode (LED), but this can only be used in *addition* to the lights mentioned above (a fact that angers many cyclists). But note that in some countries it is illegal to attach a flashing light to your bike.

3. Don't fall out of love with your brakes

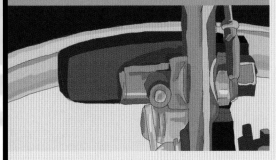

Or you'll fall *off* your bike. Your brakes are the most safety-specific part of your bike and therefore need the most care and attention. Before setting off on a ride, always make sure that all the nuts and bolts are present and correct. Work a regular brakes checklist into your maintenance routine: once a week, make sure they're working correctly; once a fortnight, look at the pads; once a month, check lubrication and for any fraying cables.

4. Don't neglect your bike's feelings

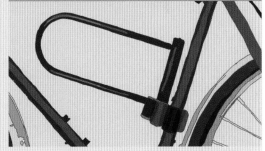

If you're spending all that time on maintenance, don't do silly things like putting your bike to one side after a wet ride – otherwise, expect rust. Wait for the weather to brighten up, then take it on a short ride to expel any water from the bearings. If you *do* find a rusty nut or bolt, soak it in oil, then try and loosen it. Another thing not to forget is security. The heavy-duty D-lock is best. Run the lock through the frame and back wheel, remove the front wheel or lock it too, then attach the lock to something immobile like a lamppost.

Take a Brake

Take care of your brakes and they'll take care of you. As brakes are the most important safety feature on your bike, they require the most maintenance. Some basic repairs – for instance, replacement of brake pads – can be carried out at home. For most other problems, seek expert advice. When it comes to brakes, it's best to swallow your amateur mechanic pride: if your attempts fail, then the consequences will be dire.

TO REPLACE A BRAKE PAD

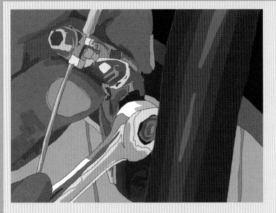

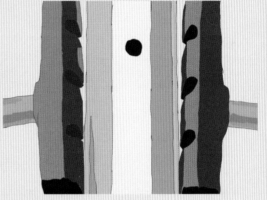

1 Loosen the nut behind the brake arm. Stop it from moving by putting an Allen key in the front of the bolt. Loosen the pad clamp.

2 Remove the pad from the clamp. Replace with a new one, positioning it as close to the rim as possible without any rubbing when the wheel is spun round. Make sure the pad is properly centred. Tighten the nut.

TO ADJUST THE CABLES

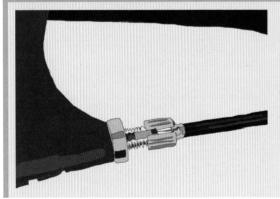

1 Locate the cable adjuster on the brake lever.

2 If the brakes are stiff, undo the nut with pliers.

3 Always leave three full threads in the lever – this will stop it from coming out.

4 At the same time, check for any fraying, rusting or general wear. Any of these factors could seriously impair the correct functioning of your brakes – something you really don't want.

Greasy Gloria

You now know that brake pads wear fast, particularly if you go on short runs in town. The same applies to the braking surface on the wall of the wheel rim – but only after serious neglect. To stop this from happening, check the surface every time you change your pads. When the surface starts wearing away, go to a mechanic and get a new wheel. Otherwise you'll run up bills for excessive brake-pad wear.

Checklist for perfect brake maintenance

- BEFORE SETTING OFF ON A RIDE: MAKE SURE YOUR BRAKES ARE WORKING CORRECTLY BY GIVING THE LEVERS A GOOD SQUEEZE. THIS SHOULDN'T TAKE MUCH EFFORT – THEY SHOULD MOVE SMOOTHLY AND QUIETLY. IF THE LEVERS END UP CLOSE TO THE BARS, THEY NEED ADJUSTING.

- ONCE A FORTNIGHT: CHECK THE PADS FOR ADJUSTMENT – THEY SHOULD FIT THE RIM CORRECTLY – AND GENERAL WEAR. PADS THAT ARE TOO WORN SLOW DOWN THE RESPONSE TIME. REMOVE ANY GRIME WITH A CLOTH.

- ALSO MAKE SURE THE CABLES AREN'T SLACK BETWEEN THE LEVER AND BRAKE MECHANISM.

- ONCE A MONTH: CHECK THE CABLES FOR SUFFICIENT LUBRICATION AND FOR ANY FRAYING, RUSTING AND GENERAL WEAR.

3 Make any fine adjustments by turning a screw at the base of the brake arm.

BRAKE LUBRICATION

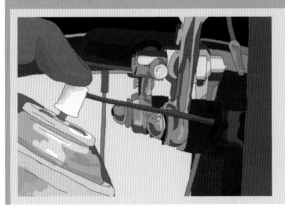

1 Use an aerosol lube – this is more accurate than oil.

2 Although lubrication varies depending on the type of brake, in general you'll need one squirt at the back of each pivot.

3 And don't forget the levers – also aim for the pivot.

4 Don't drip any lube onto the wheel rims or pads. This could damage their effectiveness.

The Wheel Thing

You'd think any problems here would be obvious – you know, your wheel's not working so your bike won't go? You're wrong. Wheel problems are stealth problems, only detected through careful vigilance. After the brakes, the wheels and tyres (see pages 124–25) are the most important components of your bike as they're the only bits that actually come into contact with the road. Most repairs require an experienced mechanic, but general maintenance can be done at home.

Maintenance checklist

- LOOK AT THE WHEEL RIMS – MAKE SURE THEY'RE CLEAN AND DENT-FREE. IF DIRTY, WIPE WITH A DRY CLOTH.

- IF YOUR WHEEL IS BENT OR DAMAGED, **DON'T RIDE YOUR BIKE**. VISIT A MECHANIC BEFORE USING IT AGAIN.

- LIKEWISE, BROKEN SPOKES SHOULD BE REFERRED TO A SPECIALIST ASAP.

- CHECK THAT YOUR WHEELS ARE 'TRUE' (IE, IN-LINE AND BALANCED). TO DO THIS: LIFT YOUR BIKE SO THE WHEEL IS OFF THE GROUND. SPIN IT AND FOCUS ON A POINT WHERE THE RIM PASSES BY ONE OF THE BRAKE PADS. IF THE RIM WOBBLES, YOUR WHEEL MAY NOT BE TRUE. SEEK A MECHANIC.

REMOVING A FRONT WHEEL

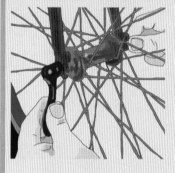

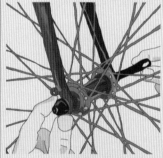

This is a million times easier if you can hang your bike up or use a work stand. If not, try and turn it upside down so it rests steadily on the saddle and handlebars.

1 Undo both nuts (anticlockwise). If your bike has quick-release levers, flip them out.

2 Free the wheel from your bike, all the while being careful not to damage the front brake pads.

To refit:

1 Reverse the above procedure, checking the rim is centred between the forks. You may have to spread the forks apart a little to ensure the lever's axle slots in correctly.

2 Make sure you fasten the levers/nuts tightly otherwise the wheel may come loose.

REMOVING A REAR WHEEL (THIS IS A LITTLE MORE TRICKY)

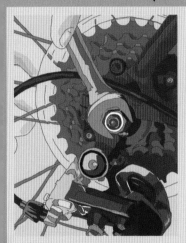  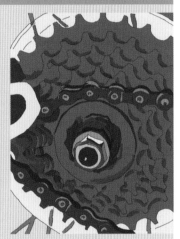

1 Find the smallest sprocket and run the chain through here. This will reduce tension on the chain.

2 Undo the nuts or lever.

3 Pull the rear mech back so the chain cage moves out of the way. This will allow the wheel to slide forward with more ease.

4 Push the wheel down and out. Not as simple as it sounds as you will have to let the rear mech return to its normal position and somehow get the chain past it. Lifting the chain from the sprocket with your fingers might help.

To refit:

1 Pull the rear mech back and slot the wheel back into place.

2 Put the chain back over the smallest sprocket.

3 Check the wheel is centred.

4 Tighten the nuts/lever.

Tyre Trouble

It was all going so well. You were happily cycling down the road and then – oops! – a pothole appears or you ride over a shard of glass or something. In any case, you now have a flat. But don't feel deflated too. Unless it's a massive gash, punctures are easy to fix. Here's how . . .

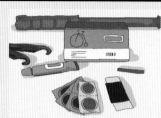
WHAT TO DO

Before even tackling a puncture, if possible remove the wheel (see previous page). This makes fixing a puncture easier. If you haven't got the necessary kit to hand, though, it's not compulsory.

Remove the tyre and tube:

1 Deflate the tyre and remove the valve nut (if your model has one).

2 Go to the opposite end of the wheel and work the tyre back and forth to free it from the rim.

3 Using the rounded end of the tyre lever, push it under the tyre bead, then yank it down to lift the bead over the rim. Try not to pinch the tube, causing additional punctures.

4 Hook the lever end onto a spoke and, about 10cm (4in) around, repeat the process with a new tyre lever. Do this with three levers – you shouldn't need any more.

5 Now go round the tyre, prising the sidewall away from the rim with your thumb.

6 Remove one of the tyre levers and run it between the rim and tyre, lifting the remaining tyre over the rim wall.

7 One side of the tyre should now be free from the rim. Reach inside and coax out the tube.

Mend the puncture:

1 Check the tube for any obvious thorns or cuts in the tread.

2 Find the puncture. The easiest way to do this is to pump the tyre up before removing it and then listen for the telltale hiss. Alternatively, take the tube out, hold it underwater – use a nearby puddle, for instance – and look for any escaping bubbles.

3 Circle the puncture with the crayon/chalk so you don't lose it.

4 Rub the area around the puncture with emery paper to remove any dirt and help the glue to bond.

Carry a spare tube with you at all times. It won't take up much space and you never know when you'll need it. Also consider investing in a spare folding tyre, available from all good bike shops. This marvellous invention will fit snugly under your saddle. And what's more, it could save you from a long walk home.

Holey war

Get far too many punctures? It could be that your tyres are simply worn out – get new ones then. Or it might be because you're not pumping your tyres up to the right pressure. Correct pressures should be between 2.1–3.4 bars (30–50psi) for mountain bikes, and between 6.2–8.3 bars (90–120psi) for 700C tyres on other bikes – consult your bike manual or dealer for precise figures. Check your pressure every fortnight.

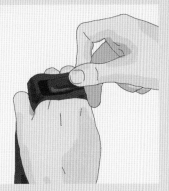
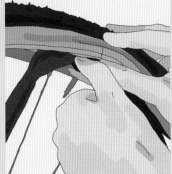

5 Apply a thin coat of glue around the puncture.

6 Leave to dry.

7 Press the patch into position, with the centre bang on top of the puncture. Smooth it out, avoiding any air bubbles. Use the end of the tyre lever to press it down firmly.

Refit the tyre and tube:

1 Inflate the tube slightly.

2 Push the section of the tube with the valve stem into the tyre and the valve stem through its hole on the rim. Don't screw on the rim nut until later.

3 Go round the wheel tucking the tube into the deepest part of the rim. Make sure it goes on evenly.

4 Next, starting at the valve, push the tyre bead over the edge of the rim. Do this all the way round the tyre. Hold the base of the valve stem clear of the rim as you do this, otherwise it might catch on the bead.

5 When the tyre is fitted neatly, pump it up.

6 Check the valve is upright, screw on the rim nut and spin the wheel round.

7 Everything should be perfect now. If not, I'm sorry, but start again.

8 If the puncture has been mended – hurrah! You can now ride off into the sunset. But after three or more punctures, it might be worth replacing the tube. After all, you never know when one of the patches will pop off . . .

Top Gears

Gears are complicated blighters. First, a recap: the two different types are derailleur and hub. Derailleurs 'derail' the chain from one sprocket to another and comprise a front mech positioned on the seat post that moves the chain between two or three chainrings, and a rear mech with up to ten sprockets. Hub gears, on the other hand, have fewer speeds and are housed within a single rear hub. Both derailleurs and hubs operate via cables connected to the gear shifters on the handlebars. As hubs are hidden, both maintenance and repairs should be left to the professionals. However, since they're lower maintenance, problems should be rare.

 Greasy Gloria

Clean and lube the gears and shifters every time you service the chain – anywhere between two weeks and once a month should be enough. If you don't fancy mucky hands, wear latex gloves.

DERAILLEUR FRONT MECH

Maintenance:

Check, clean and lubricate at least once a month. It's also worth quickly checking over the front mech before each ride. Here's how:

1 Lift your rear wheel off the ground.

2 Turn the pedals and shift your front gear lever through its entire range. The chain should move smoothly from one ring to the next.

Any problems? You may have to give the mech a good clean and lube.

1 Clean it with a stiff brush or a rag soaked in degreaser.

2 Use a spray lubricant on the pivots.

3 Wipe off any excess as this will only attract dirt.

Still struggling? Try readjusting the mech:

To position:

1 Shift the arm over the largest chainring. The cage should be 2mm (½in) above the teeth of the chainring. The chain and cage ring should run parallel. If not, loosen the cable fixing bolt and move the chain to the smallest chainring. Adjust the screw marked 'L' until there's a 2mm (½in) gap.

2 Pull the cable and tighten the bolt. Then move the chain to the largest chainring and adjust the screw marked 'H' for a 2mm (½in) gap.

To reposition:

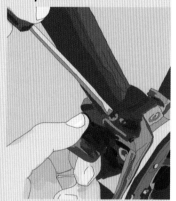

1 Loosen the mounting bolt.

2 Reposition the mech by sliding it up and down. You may need to loosen the cable to do this.

3 When the mech is correctly repositioned, retighten the mounting bolt.

CABLES

If damaged, frayed or over-worn, the gear cables must be changed. This is another tricky job best left to a professional. Most cable problems, however, merely require adjusting, as the cables must be correctly tensioned to work effectively. To do this:

1 Find the barrel adjuster, usually located at the point where the gear lever cable meets the lever. Use this to increase or decrease the tension in your cable.

2 Start with the chain on the largest front ring and largest rear sprocket. Then shift the chain down to the next chainring. Look to see how close the inside surface of the chain is to the inside wall of the front mech cage (they should be almost touching).

3 Turn the barrel adjuster anticlockwise to move the cage away from the chain surface. Then turn it clockwise.

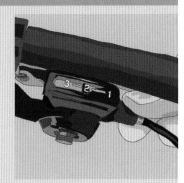

DERAILLEUR REAR MECH

This is MUCH more temperamental.

Maintenance:

Like the front mech, check, clean and lubricate at least once a month. It's also worth checking over before each ride. To do this:

1 Suspend the rear wheel off the ground.

2 Spin the pedals while moving the rear shift lever through all its gearing options. The chain should move easily from sprocket to sprocket.

Any problems? Dirt may be the cause . . .

Clean and lubricate:

1 Clean and lube in the same way as a front mech, paying particular attention to the jockey wheels (in the cage of the mech).

2 At the same time inspect the jockey wheels – this is the bit that wears out fastest. Pull the chain cage forward, and wiggle the jockey to test for movement and to see if it turns freely.

Still not working? Try a minor adjustment . . .

To adjust:

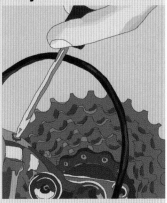

1 Move the chain to the smallest sprocket. Undo the cable fixing clamp and turn the 'H' screw until the jockey wheels are inline with the smallest sprocket. Tighten the cable.

2 Move the chain to the largest sprocket and push the rear mech to see if it travels further than this sprocket. If it does, turn the 'L' screw until it aligns.

3 If this fails, take your bike to a mechanic.

Chain Reaction

Cycle-philes often refer to the chain as the heart of the bike. Sounds soppy, we know, but like the heart, the chain needs special care and attention, especially if you're riding on a daily basis. A clean, well-maintained chain means a bike that runs smoothly. After all, it's thanks to the chain that your bike actually moves. Remember, because the chain connects all the major components of your drivetrain, it can thus distribute your leg muscle power through these components to produce a forward momentum. And get you moving.

Maintenance

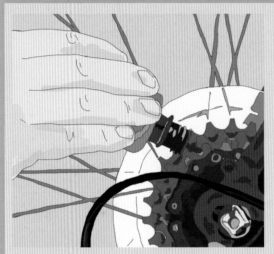

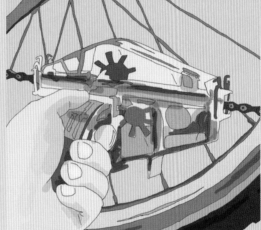

Before every ride:
Give your chain a quick once-over to make sure it's clean and lubricated.

Once a fortnight:
Look for wear and tight links.

1 Turn the pedals slowly backwards.

2 Look at each of the chain links for any dirt or tight links.

Every month:
Give it a quick clean.

1 Remember to put lots of newspaper down – cleaning your chain could get messy.

2 Use a chain cleaner (available from all good bike shops and designed to cause as little mess as possible) or a toothbrush and solvent. Wash off with plenty of water. Use a cloth to wipe the chainrings.

3 Once dried, use a lubricant specifically designed for chains. Wipe off any excess lube.

4 While servicing your chain, check over your cranks and chainrings for damage or for loose bolts.

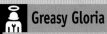
If your chain isn't running smoothly, tight links could be to blame. They're easy to spot: turn your pedals slowly backwards and carefully inspect your chain. A good clean and lube routine should sort out the problem, or try jiggling the links with your hands. If this doesn't work, the chain could be damaged and should be replaced.

HOW TO REMOVE YOUR CHAIN

1 First you must figure out what kind of chain you're dealing with. There are two types. The kind used on bikes with non-derailleur gears is held together with a master link. To undo the chain, pull the master link apart with your fingers.

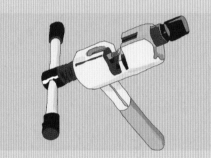

2 The other type, found on bikes with derailleur gears, has no master link. The chain must therefore be taken apart with a special chain riveting tool.

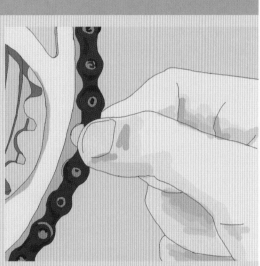

Every couple of months:
Give it a thorough clean.

1 Remove the chain from your bike (see right).

2 Scrub thoroughly with a chain cleaner or toothbrush.

3 Leave to soak overnight in degreaser.

4 Dry using a clean cloth. Inspect for general wear.

5 Lubricate and refit.

Also remember to check for chain stretch:
Lift one link of the chain away from the front chainring. If there's a visible gap between the chain and chainring, replace the chain.

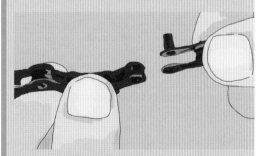

3 Make sure the tool's point centres exactly on the rivet. Tighten the handle in a clockwise direction and push the rivet out, but not all the way out – go only as far as the outside plate.

Use Your Head

Your headset is made up of the top and bottom ball bearings at the front of your bike; both are pressed into the head tube. The headset essentially allows your handlebars, stem and fork to move smoothly.

 Greasy Gloria

Remember to check the handlebars for cracks and make sure the bolts are tight. And don't forget the bolt on the stem: this must be tight enough to stop the handlebars from moving in the frame.

CHECKING YOUR HEADSET

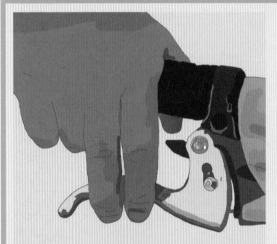

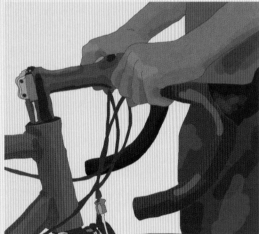

Many riders don't think that it's necessary to check the headset. This is a mistake as the headset must be in tip-top condition for trouble-free steering. Also, because the headset is subjected to such high pressures, it can deteriorate very quickly, so any signs that there is something not quite right need to be attended to immediately. Although you can do the following inspections at home, it's best to leave anything more advanced to the professionals.

The saddle is another component that is often overlooked. Check the seat post bolt is tight (where the saddle tube meets the main cycle frame) and look out for any cracks. Ensure that the clip underneath the saddle isn't damaging the seat post.

Checklist:

Before every ride:
Squeeze the front brake and rock the bike backwards and forwards. If you can hear a clicking sound in the headset, the bearings are loose. If so, consult a mechanic.

And every so often:
Check your bearing systems. Lift the front wheel off the ground and turn the handlebars slowly and gradually, backwards and forwards. This operation should be super-smooth.

Lights Fantastic

When riding at night, being seen by other road users is not only a legal requirement, it's also essential for your own safety. There are lots of different types of front and rear lights on the market, the best being those that incorporate a halogen bulb (similar to the ones used in car headlights, only smaller). Although battery-powered lights are more expensive than the dynamo variety (which act like a mini power station fitted to your wheel), you can remove them and put in your bag when you're not with your bike. In other words, they're thief-proof.

MAKE SURE YOU'RE SEEN

Greasy Gloria

In the UK it is a legal requirement to have a white reflector at the front and a red reflector at the rear. The rear reflector can be part of the rear light itself. Reflectors are essential for night riding and a necessary backup for lights. Also recommended: wheel and pedal reflectors, plus reflective leg- and armbands. Basically, buy some self-adhesive reflective tape, and stick it everywhere you can!

Battery-powered lights may be cheaper to buy, but those powered by a dynamo will be cheaper in the long run. On the down side, a dynamo rubs against your wheel and can be a bit annoying.

Before riding at night, check your lights are working at full power. Any problems and you may need to change the batteries. If there's still a problem, remove the batteries and check for any green-coloured gunk. Scrape it out with a screwdriver, then spray on some lubricant.

Always carry spare bulbs when riding at night. The super-cautious should consider a spare battery, too.

Grime Stoppers: Keeping Your Bike Clean

Consider a good wash and lube routine for your bike in the same way you might religiously cleanse, tone and moisturise your face. You can't expect a happy, healthy complexion if you go to bed with a face-full of slap; likewise, leaving a bike muddy will affect its performance. A bike needs cleaning at least once a month. Lubricate (moisturise) the chain once a fortnight, the rest of the bike monthly. If it's raining a lot, do lube more often. It's worth it.

WASHING UP

Kit:
- BOTTLE BRUSH

- WASHING-UP BRUSH

- TOOTHBRUSH

- SPONGE

- CHAMOIS LEATHER

- VARIOUS BIKE WASHES/CLEANSERS INCLUDING A WATER-DISPENSING LUBE, WASHING-UP LIQUID AND A WATER-SOLUBLE DEGREASER

1 Wash the bike with washing-up liquid and a sponge. Don't use a pressure washer – this will be too powerful for a bike – and if using a hose, apply the water gently. A bucket is best. Use a water-soluble degreaser on the mechs and chainwheel.

2 Wash the bike again, this time using the bottlebrush and toothbrush to remove dirt from any awkward nooks and crannies.

3 Rinse and then dry with a chamois leather.

4 The washing-up liquid may make the frame streaky, but a bike polish will bring back its shine.

Make the most of bath-time. Washing your bike is the ideal opportunity to keep an eye out for any repairs that might need doing. Also look for hairline cracks in the frame or any wobbly nuts and bolts that can be fixed super-sharp before they cause an accident. Those suds could stop a nasty thud.

LUBING DOWN

Do this after every wash, but don't be over-zealous. Wipe off any excess lube as it can easily attract dirt.

Where do I lube?
Aim for any moving parts and cable points.

What lube should I choose?
There are scores of options on the market. Common-or-garden oil is good, but it attracts dirt. Dry lubricant in aerosol form is better – it will leave behind a solid lubricant when it evaporates, plus it reaches the hard-to-get spots. Use a water-dispensing lubricant after riding in the rain. You need grease for the bearings. Use a specially formulated lube for the chain.

BRAKE LEVERS	BRAKE PIVOTS/ CANTILEVERS	INNER CABLES	FRONT MECH
		 (image)	(image)
Squirt aerosol lubricant on the pivots, the inner cable, the cable adjusters and the gear shifters.	The pivots need some grease as well as a squirt of spray lube. The cantilevers also need some lube.	Squirt lube at the cable points.	Aim for the pivots.

CHAIN AND SPROCKETS	REAR MECH	JOCKEY WHEELS	V-BRAKE
			(image)
The most important part of your lubricating routine. Wipe off the dirt and then lube.	One squirt on each pivot.	Squirt the bearings.	The pivots need a squirt of spray lube; likewise the cable attachments, but less frequently.

Ready, Steady . . . Go! The Ten-minute Road Check

Do this as often as you can – it's best to know if something's wrong before setting out. Any problems, and flip back through this book for possible solutions.

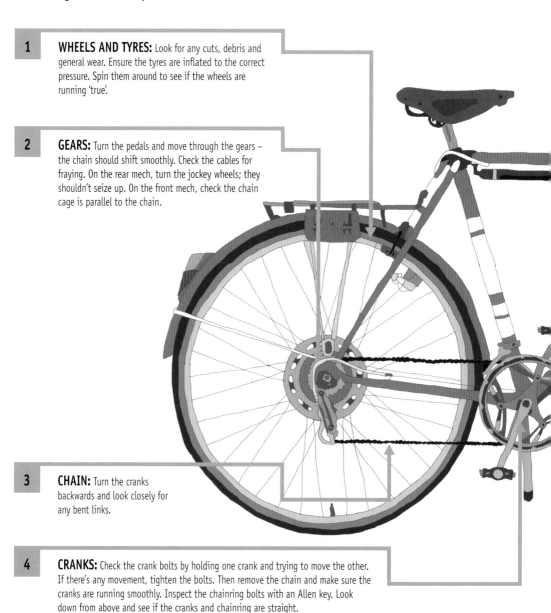

1 **WHEELS AND TYRES:** Look for any cuts, debris and general wear. Ensure the tyres are inflated to the correct pressure. Spin them around to see if the wheels are running 'true'.

2 **GEARS:** Turn the pedals and move through the gears – the chain should shift smoothly. Check the cables for fraying. On the rear mech, turn the jockey wheels; they shouldn't seize up. On the front mech, check the chain cage is parallel to the chain.

3 **CHAIN:** Turn the cranks backwards and look closely for any bent links.

4 **CRANKS:** Check the crank bolts by holding one crank and trying to move the other. If there's any movement, tighten the bolts. Then remove the chain and make sure the cranks are running smoothly. Inspect the chainring bolts with an Allen key. Look down from above and see if the cranks and chainring are straight.

Greasy Gloria

Think about your pedals. You need good ones, yet most bike manufacturers will fob you off with the cheapest models possible. If yours don't seem up to scratch, replace them with pedals that have a decent cage and good bearings. Don't skimp on maintenance either; clean and lubricate regularly. Creaking pedals could mean the bearings in the crank are dry. Remove the pedal and grease the axle and its ball bearings.

HEADSET: Look for any cracks. Any wobbles between the forks and the frame mean the headset needs adjusting. **5**

BRAKES: Make sure they're properly adjusted. Squeeze the levers – the brakes should be fully on when you squeeze them halfway down. The brake pads should not be worn. The cables must not be frayed. **6**

LIGHTS AND REFLECTORS: Make sure your lights are working at full power. If you need to change a bulb, avoid touching the glass directly – use a piece of tissue or cloth to hold it in place. **7**

FRAME: Look for any cracks. Also check the saddle is secure. **8**

How To Be a Savvy Cyclist

Although this book is about maintenance and repairs, to survive on the road you also need some cycling know-how. Think of the following as a short lesson in cycling proficiency.

Practice makes perfect

Unlike motorists and bikers, cyclists aren't required to have lessons or pass a test. But a reckless cyclist can be a menace to other road users; likewise, an inexperienced cyclist can feel threatened and intimidated. If you're nervous about cycling in traffic, practise beforehand in a vehicle-free environment (for example, an empty car park). Hold the handlebars firmly and relax your shoulders. Make sure you're familiar with all the correct hand signals. And remember, when you turn, to keep your outside pedal the nearest one to the ground.

Defensive cycling

The two key principles to being a good rider are defensive and assertive cycling. Defensive cycling means being hyper-aware of what's going on around you at all times – fixing mirrors to your handlebars can help with rear vision. You must anticipate the worst case scenario. Imagine that the car ahead will swerve, for instance, or a pedestrian will jump out in front of you. Look ahead for such nasties as manhole covers and potholes. You should avoid riding over them, but should also avoid having to swerve to do so. The most important thing is to be on guard at all times.

 Greasy Gloria

The super-sussed cyclist is always prepared, ever ready for the unexpected. Think about the following before setting off and your ride should be blissfully uneventful:

- **Plan your route beforehand: this way you will be focused on the road, and not deliberating the correct turning.**

- **Be prepared: carry a spare tube, a pump and a puncture repair kit.**

- **Invest in a water bottle: cycling can be thirsty work.**

- **Don't carry a passenger unless you have a passenger seat.**

- **And finally, don't carry anything that might affect your balance or become entangled in your wheels.**

Get to grip with your gears. Make sure you're familiar with when to go high – and when to go low. For example, move into a low gear before stopping. Flat, smooth surfaces on the other hand, require you to engage higher gears.

Assertive cycling

Assertive cycling means making others aware of you, and this is where confidence comes in handy. Ride in the correct place on the road in single file so other vehicles can pass safely – and don't ride on the pavement. Make clear movements; don't make sudden turns. Don't ride up close behind another vehicle. And always, always, obey traffic law: traffic signs don't apply only to motorists.

A good cyclist will play the flirt and make regular eye contact with other road users. This confirms your presence. Once eye contact is established, glance in the direction you're going, while making the appropriate hand signal. This is especially important when navigating roundabouts.

Cyclists can sometimes use bus lanes, but only if the sign includes a cycle symbol. When riding in a bus lane, be very aware of the bus – people getting off it, the bus stopping and starting, and so forth. So many accidents happen this way.

Cycling in bad weather

Riding in bad weather requires caution. Go slowly and think before you act. Again, prepare for the worst. If the forecast predicts rain, carry some waterproof gear and watch out for road markings – they can become very slippery. Be particularly cautious in an urban area if you're riding in rain after a dry spell – since the water mixes with any oil spillages on the road, the surface swiftly becomes akin to an ice rink. Move ahead with caution.

If it's cold, consider layers – fleeces of varying degrees of thickness work well – and gloves. Fog and ice are both extremely cyclist-unfriendly, so avoid if possible – it's really not worth the risk.

Whatever the weather, though, remember to make yourself visible. Never neglect your lights and reflectors.

Learn the Lingo

Hmmmm. You've been studying this book, waving your monkey wrench around, but you still can't get your bike to work? Since we only deal with basic repairs, you'll now need professional help. But unless you know the right lingo, visiting a workshop – one of the last bastions of maleness – could be fraught with difficulties.

Cycling requires learning a whole new language. Can you differentiate your crank from your chainring? Know the exact meaning – or, indeed, location – of a jockey wheel? Exactly. Read on if you want to avoid getting shafted by a mean mechanic.

Dealing with the professionals

The best mechanic is one that's been recommended by a trusted acquaintance. If, however, none of your friends knows anyone, shop around for the best quote. You shouldn't be charged for the initial examination. Ask for a written quotation before work gets started.

Find out the price of any bike parts that need replacing – go to a good cycle shop or call your bicycle manufacturer to ask the recommended retail price – that way you'll know if you're paying over the odds for professional repairs. Another tip is to ask the mechanic to give you the old parts back when your bike is returned. Just to make sure you're actually getting new parts.

Go through the bill carefully. Make sure it is itemised and query any additional costs. If you're unhappy, it's best to clear the thing up right away.

Finally, always remember to weigh up the pros and cons of getting expensive work done to your bike. It might just be cheaper to get a new one.

Parlez-vous bike?

A BRIEF GLOSSARY OF TECHNICAL TERMS.

Allen key
A six-sided, L-shaped slot-in tool that comes in a set of varying sizes; good for adjustments to recessed bolts.

Brake pads
Rubber pads that touch the wheel rim when the brake lever is applied.

Bead
The specially strengthened edge of the tyre. When the tyre is inflated, this holds it to the wheel rim.

Bearings
Minimise friction between fixed and moving bike parts.

Cantilever brakes
When applied, they squeeze the wheel rim (the part of the wheel closest to the tyre).

Cassette
A collection of sprockets found on the rear wheel.

Chain cage
On the rear mech, this consists of two jockey wheels and side plates. Its function is to regulate the chain tension.

Chainring
The toothed wheel in the chainset that is attached to the right-hand crank and works with the chain.

Chainset
The collective name for the chainrings and cranks.

Chainwheel
Another name for the chainring.

Cranks
Arms that connect the pedals to the main frame.

Drivetrain
The combination of pedals, chain, chainset and sprockets, which together drive the bike forward when pedal power is applied.

Derailleur gear
A gearing system that moves the chain from one sprocket to another (at rear) and one chainring to another (at front).

Dynamo
A battery-free light that is powered by the bike's momentum.

Front mech (front gear mechanism)
Part of the derailleur gearing system. A metal 'cage' attached to the seat post that moves the chain between two or three chainrings.

Headset
Two sets of ball bearings located above and below the frame's head tube. This helps the bike steering.

Hub gears
A type of gearing system. The gearing mechanism is built into the hub (centre) of the rear wheel.

Hub-mounted brakes
When applied, the brakes squeeze the wheel's hub (the centre).

Jockey wheels
The small wheels in the chain cage of the rear mech. This guides the chain round the sprockets.

Mudguards
Partly cover the bike's wheels to stop mud splattering the rider.

Pannier
A holdall that fits onto a cycle rack, usually at the rear of the bike.

Rear mech (rear gear mechanism)
Part of the derailleur gearing system.

Rim-mounted brakes
When applied, they squeeze the wheel rim (the part of the wheel closest to the tyre).

Seat post
The tube that supports the saddle.

Sprocket
A toothed wheel that transfers drive (your pedal power) from the chain to the centre of the bike's wheel.

Torque wrench
A specially designed wrench that makes a loud click when the exact amount of force required for the nut and bolt has been applied, preventing you from over- or under-tightening the joint.

Tyre levers
Small levers crucial for removing and refitting a tube and tyre.

Touring and Going Abroad

In bicycle-mad places like Holland, 27 per cent of all holidays are by bike. The clued-up Dutch know it's healthy, a pleasant way to see sights and relatively stress-free.

It's worth bearing in mind the type of bike you ride: can it cope on uncertain terrain? Will it be comfortable over long distances? Flip back to pages 108–09 for more information on the different types of bicycles available. It might be wise investing in a new one, and if not a new bike, then perhaps a new saddle or some cycle-specific clothes such as lycra shorts and cycling shoes.

The other factor that requires careful thought is your route. Plan your journey in as much detail as possible before setting off. It will be easier – and more enjoyable – if you concentrate on smaller roads with less traffic and bridleways (legal 'footpaths' for cyclists). For

First aid kit

WHETHER POOTLING DOWN A COUNTRY LANE OR INDULGING IN SOME SERIOUS OFF-ROAD ACTION, A FIRST AID KIT IS CRUCIAL. ALWAYS INCLUDE THE FOLLOWING:

- Plasters in a variety of shapes and sizes
- Bandages
- Scissors
- Surgical tape
- Antiseptic wipes

Essential touring kit

WHETHER YOU'RE SPENDING AN AFTERNOON CRUISING ROUND YOUR LOCAL COUNTRYSIDE, OR A SUMMER DOING FRANCE, YOU'LL NEED TO PACK CERTAIN ITEMS. THE FOLLOWING LIST SHOULD GIVE YOU SOME IDEA:

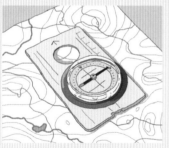

- First aid kit (see right)
- Tool kit plus spare parts – take as much as you can carry
- Blanket
- Water and food

- Map
- Compass
- Penknife and/or multi-tool
- Suitable clothing including cold weather and raingear

overseas travel, make sure you understand the road signs and highway codes of the country you're visiting.

Another problem, unless you intend cycling the entire journey, is transporting your bike. A huge variety of bike racks for cars are now available. Most are secured to the car roof while some are attached to the boot. If using a boot rack, bear in mind you may have to buy an extra set of plates and lights as they could become obscured.

Beware of the dog

Touring requires a whole host of new cycling skills. One particular hassle most urban cyclists are woefully unprepared for is the presence of animals. If you spot a dog off its lead, for instance, stop riding, and if the dog becomes aggressive, put your bike between the two of you. Also be wary of horses – approach them slowly from behind and make sure the rider is fully aware of your presence.

Going off-road

The more adventurous cyclist may be tempted with off-road riding, undoubtedly the best way to be at one with nature. Again, packing is crucial: you will need waterproofs, fleeces, food and drink, a compass and a survival bag. Novices should stick to special off-road tracks at a mountain bike centre until they become more confident.

Finally, all touring cyclists, whatever the level, should pay particular attention to cleaning and lubrication, especially if your bike is usually only used to city streets. Get on your bike – what are you waiting for?

Carrying a load

Inanimate loads

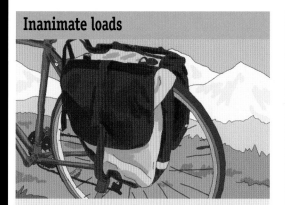

Backpacks, unless small, aren't a good idea. Clever cyclists tend to move their load onto their bike rack; this is more comfortable and more stable as it lowers the centre of gravity.

There are several different types of cycle bags on the market, the most popular being the handlebar bag, the saddlebag and the pannier. Trailers are another option and particularly good for overall balance. Whatever method you decide on, you should remember when packing to start with the heaviest gear at the bottom, and split the load between the front and rear of the bike. Never overload your bike as this could affect its balance. Get used to the new weight by going on a practice ride.

It's also worth investing in a handlebar bag so you can easily dip in for your essentials – map, money, etc – without unpacking the rest of your luggage.

When carrying a load, don't neglect your bike maintenance. Check the forks and frame more regularly as the extra weight can cause extra stress.

And don't forget security. When parking your bike, keep your belongings secure. Better still, take them with you.

Very animate loads

What about loads of the human variety?

Like bags, child carriers come in a wide range of styles and sizes – you can even buy ones that recline, which is great for sleepy children. Most attach to the rear cycle rack, while some attach to the top tube, making them brilliant for communication.

Trailers are another mode of transportation and are ideal for toddlers who have out-grown their child seats. The next stage up is trailer bikes that you attach to the back of your bike – the perfect introduction to 'proper' cycling.

Always make sure that your child is strapped in securely and kitted out in suitable clothing for the cycling and weather conditions. Stop frequently for drink and food breaks – a grumpy child will be no fun.

And whatever you do, don't forget a helmet. Choose one that protects the ears as this guarantees more protection for the head, although children on trailer bikes should wear helmets without ear protection to enable them to hear any instructions. Since children must hold their heads up while wearing a helmet, experts generally advise against putting a child under the age of one on a bike. Save the treat for a little later in life.

Index

DO YOU KNOW IT ALL ALREADY? QUIZ ANSWERS

WHAT IS A SALOON?

A A type of car distinguished by its separate boot

FROM WHAT IS COOLANT COMPOSED?

C One-third anti-freeze and two-thirds water

HOW OFTEN SHOULD YOU CLEAN YOUR MOTORCYCLE?

C Fortnightly

WHAT DOES AN ODOMETER MEASURE?

B The number of kilometres/miles a car has driven

WHAT'S THE BEST BRUSH FOR CLEANING A BICYCLE?

D A toothbrush

WHAT IS A TORQUE WRENCH?

A A tool that makes a loud click when the correct amount of pressure is applied to a nut and bolt

WHAT ARE THE BEST SHOES FOR CYCLING?

C Trainers

WHEN CARRYING A PASSENGER ON A MOTORCYCLE, WHAT'S THE MOST IMPORTANT PIECE OF INFORMATION TO TELL THEM ABOUT BEFORE SETTING OFF?

A Lean into bends